MARRYING OU
YOUR TRADI

MARRYING OUTSIDE YOUR TRADITION

A Practical and Spiritual Guide

REV. DR. DONNA SCHAPER

ROWMAN & LITTLEFIELD
Lanham • Boulder • New York • London

Published by Rowman & Littlefield
An imprint of The Rowman & Littlefield Publishing Group, Inc.
4501 Forbes Boulevard, Suite 200, Lanham, Maryland 20706
www.rowman.com

86-90 Paul Street, London EC2A 4NE

Copyright © 2023 by The Rowman & Littlefield Publishing Group, Inc.

British Library Cataloguing in Publication Information Available

Library of Congress Cataloging-in-Publication Data

978-1-5381-4352-0 (cloth)
978-1-5381-4353-7 (electronic)

CONTENTS

INTRODUCTION

"I'M IN LOVE WITH SOMEONE OUTSIDE MY TRADITION. SHOULD I panic or enjoy or take turns worrying and enjoying?" I first heard this question in a course I taught at New York University, a hotbed of international life if there ever was one. The course was requested by the chaplains there. It was called "Dating Outside Your Tribe." We had six couples in the first course. One was a Hindu/Muslim couple from the northern part of the country of India. They were thinking of marriage. They also knew they could never go home. One or both might be killed. That level of traditional religion was a surprise to the other five couples. But they got the point. There is a remarkable social freedom in even being able to date outside your tradition. Another of the couples was Jewish and Christian, a third two women, one with parents who disapproved of her sexual orientation. A fourth was an evangelical trying to understand her progressive Christian husband. They were, in my view, the least likely to succeed. Her absolutism and his relativity were not going to be friends for long. The fifth couple were two men, one of whom wanted a marriage with sexual freedom; the other did not. And the sixth couple was an upper-class Jew and a working-class Jew. They also knew their differences more than their similarities quite well. I learned a lot from this little six-week course, much of which will show up in this book.

I have also been a parish pastor for almost fifty years and have officiated around five hundred weddings, most of which have been interfaith, interracial, secular/religious, or mixed up or "miscegenated" in some way. Every now and then I get two Lutherans or two Catholics. I have developed a curriculum for premarital counseling, which this book comes from. This ministry of intimate diversity has shown me the "new field" of postsecularism, which of course includes religious backgrounds. It also reminds me of my favorite quote from Persian Muslim poet Rumi. He said, "There is a field out beyond the field of right and wrong. Come out. I'll meet you there."

Yes, traditional religion is in hospice. It is on its way out. Fewer and fewer people will observe traditional religious practices or want to marry inside their tradition. The trend is clear.

New forms of spiritual experience populate birthing rooms and wedding venues, which include fewer sacred sites. Marriage is sacramentally stranded and religiously homeless. People audaciously write their own vows. Many people promise different things to each other. Marriage is simultaneously a place of intimate experimentation with the holy and a site of confusion, if not difficulty and danger. How do we raise the children? When we date or marry outside our traditions, we live intimate lives of spiritual exploration. I applaud (and evaluate) our efforts at living sacramentally in post-religious, postsecular, *spiritual* ways.

Here I offer a practical and spiritual guide to the old ways of marriage and the new ones. I appreciate them each and all—and want to particularly address people who are spiritually stranded by their faiths of origin and alert to new revelations through their own intimate experience. Straight and gay, Jewish and Christian, none of the above, and evangelicals will find a way to think about the loves of their lives in tribal and posttribal ways. Think of this book as spiritual preparation for something no one knows much about *yet*.

I start with how religion has changed and how therefore we have changed. I conclude with a guide to having more agency in what kind of religious experience you use to support your own life and its loves.

Beginning with how religion has changed and how marriage has changed, I talk about how change is the only constant matter. We don't have choice so much as evolution. The species is obviously moving to a more mixed-race, mixed-religion, mixed-upness.

I believe and will argue here that this is God's destination for the world. A friend of mine quipped, "I wish we were all already all brown." I think God intends our motion beyond the tribal—and that the creator intends for us to eventually be all mixed up. Rituals and their tribes and their ancient texts truly matter and are truly wonderful—and they are rapidly changing.

When the book moves to the more practical and less spiritual and theological parts, I look at dating rituals and mores, at wedding ceremonies, at divorce, at children, and stepchildren and stepparenting. Who ever thought they'd find the love of their life online? It will move back and forth between the practical and the spiritual because they are so fundamentally connected.

In both the practical and the spiritual parts, I emphasize appreciation of change and curiosity about it. My goal is to equip the reader to be a change agent and not be overwhelmed by the mixed-upness of intimate life, with families of origin, current partners, and children's religious and spiritual preparation. Think mother-in-law jokes and how to move beyond them.

Of course, marriage is a site of conflict. It is a site of conflict because it is a site of love. You can't have love without conflict— and intermarriage creates even more conflict for marriages than marriages within the tribe do. I often say in premarital and marital counseling, after the inevitable troubles begin, that marriage is the art of balancing power. If both partners feel powerful and in charge, they will be very happy together. If one gets too big, or the other too small, watch out. They will figure out how to make each other miserable. That truth about marriage existed before people married so frequently outside their tribes. It is only more true as cultural proficiency becomes an added skill people need to accompany their power-filled selves. Thus, this book, which loves the love—and its complications—that exist post tribally.

It is a guide to becoming happily miscegenated. This guide loves it when all things are mixed up, even lovers. It blesses mixed-race children. It will help increase the likelihood that you will be happily married and raise happy children. It will decrease your chances of divorcing. One out of two marriages today ends in divorce. Interfaith and interracial marriages have a higher percentage of divorce. They are likewise becoming increasingly common. Why not learn how to be happily married before you have trouble or are surprised about what marriage outside your tribe means to the wider earth or to your in-laws? How can you be ready to live a life of intimate diversity? How will you raise the children or manage your in-laws? Do you really think God's purpose in history is to blend races and religions? Do you think intermarriage is an evolution or devolution? What will happen to your tribe if you marry out? What prejudices do you bring about Jews or Christians or Muslims—or none of the above? How do you care about that? What are the opportunities and problems involved with raising children when you and your spouse are different parents?

How do we create institutions that support us? What kind of wedding service is ideal for a mixed-race or mixed-religion couple? What about secular couples who really do live "beyond" religion? What if God has nothing to do with any of this? What does that mean after all these years of thinking of marriage as a sacrament? How do you stay ready for surprises, the good ones and the ones that cause you to suffer?

This book will also be a short course in living culturally in a world that is tipping to mixed families. Even if you are in a tribal-friendly marriage or family, you may want to know how to relate to others who are not. My eleven-year-old grandson just told me he is in love with a person who is a them.

Yup, and they are their first love.

We can't really help falling in love with someone who is different from us. We can help ourselves enjoy diversity.

1

Marriage and Religious Change

RELATIONSHIPS ARE CHANGING IN AMERICA—AND SO IS MAR-riage. In fact, there are dramatic shifts in recent decades that forecast even more changes in the decades ahead. This book is a positive look at those changes. It affirms the changes while developing empathy for those who are the trailblazers and path makers. There is nothing easy about doing something "new," especially in the world where religious tradition rules. Consider this practical and spiritual guide as a midcourse adjustment, an intermediate stop on the long road of human evolution, with hope for excellent things to come out of change.

Religion: that which binds us to a culture, to a picture of God, and to the generations before us and those coming. Religion comes from *religare*, a Latin word meaning "to bind." Religion creates a long sense of belonging, reaching deep into the human past. It also thrusts belonging far into the future. It is not an accident that Ancestry.com is the most popular web destination of all, second only to pornography. We want to know who "our people" are. We want to know about our past. We don't want to be chained to it so much as acquainted with it.

Marriage: a sacred promise to partner with another forever. "Till death do us part" means that we are free to marry again when the first partner dies, leaving the other alone. But it also promises thick and thin, richer or poorer, sickness and in health as long as we are alive and still promised legally and morally to each other. These are big promises to belong, as unconditionally as possible, to one other.

When I was a child, fifty years ago, when people divorced, they were looked down upon. Today, divorce happens in one out of two marriages, and judgment is withheld. We morally "permit" divorce while still encouraging marriage. This is a sea change in my lifetime: from religious judgment to a kind of spiritual permission. Marriage and the concept of forever have divorced. Serial marriage is permitted, although people do start to frown a bit after the second.

Religion changed in many more ways than just divorcing forever in marriage. Marriage also changed in ways still inscrutable for the plain fact that we don't have statistics for what was before to compare what we see now. But half of us, including me, have known the agony of divorce or at least the loss of a former intimate. Divorce is not desirable so much as normalized.

People also marry older. In 2017, half of Americans ages eighteen and older were married, a share that has remained stable in recent years but starting trending up 8 percentage points since 1990. More people stayed single longer.

Divorce rates have also increased among older Americans. People still marry for what they call love. But one in two marriages also end in divorce. Older Americans are divorcing at triple the rate since 1990.[1]

The moral landscape of relationships in America has shifted dramatically in recent decades. More people "live together" before formally marrying. They behave as married couples but are not legally married. Parents of my generation permit cohabitation in our own homes, without a comment. Virginity is more a joke than a moral complaint or virtue.

From cohabitation to same-sex marriage to interracial and interethnic marriage, here are some facts about love and marriage in the United States. More people are living together. Remarriage is on the rise. One in six newlyweds (17 percent) were married to someone of a different race or ethnicity in 2015. There have been steady increases in intermarriage since 1967, when just 3 percent of people were intermarried.

While Asian (29 percent) and Hispanic (27 percent) newlyweds are most likely to intermarry in the US, the most dramatic increases in intermarriage have occurred among black newlyweds, 18 percent of whom married someone of a different race or ethnicity, up from 5 percent in 1980. About one in ten white newlyweds (11 percent) are married to someone of a different race or ethnicity.

Among both Gen Zers and millennials, 53 percent say people of different races marrying each other is a good thing for our society, compared with 41 percent of Gen Xers, 30 percent of boomers, and 20 percent of those in the silent generation.[2]

Simultaneously, support for the legalization of same-sex marriage has grown in the past ten years, with millennials and Generation Z leading that pack as well.

Interestingly, all this diversity appreciation breaks down at the level of political affiliation.

About four in ten Americans who have married since 2010 (39 percent) have a spouse who is in a different religious group, compared with only 19 percent of those who wed before 1960.[3] Many of these interfaith marriages are between Christians and those who are religiously unaffiliated.[4]

When it comes to politics, a 2016 Pew Research Center survey found that 77 percent of both Republicans and Democrats who were married or living with a partner said their spouse or partner was in the same party.[5]

When I was a child, I witnessed my parents look down on people who divorced. Moreover, I heard them sneer about a Protestant marrying a Catholic or a Catholic marrying a Jew. Marriage outside of the religious tradition was considered ill-advised and not just because the couple might have trouble on weekends figuring out how to worship. One tradition often thought itself the superior to the other, religiously. They weren't kidding.

The current orthodoxy about marriage, beyond horror by Democratic parents if a child dates a Republican and vice versa, is around class. We are instructed by dating sites to list our preferred income level of a preferred date way before they want to know our religious instructions.

Some even argue that algorithms are a new form of arranged marriage. We list our criteria; the potential applicant lists his or her or their criteria. Yes, even pronouns are changing to include people who identify as transitioned or in transition. We then approve and test each other, but the potential partner has been preapproved, as it were, by a digital tradition.

These budding criteria for dating, then marriage, all make one of the largest points of all. Marrying inside a tradition of similarity, of class, race, or religion, will likely be more successful than marrying outside of these similarities. By successful, we mean the relationship lasting. People don't marry to get divorced. They marry to get married, to live long and happy together. Marriage counselors, like myself, know to make this point. The more the difference, the higher the divorce rates. There is a lot of territory to travel when we don't come shaped the same. Not to mention the very important question of what happens to the children. Do they go to Hebrew school or Sunday school? Are they confirmed, baptized, or do they have a bris?

Ask Meghan Markle what it is like to marry outside the tradition. Or Romeo or Juliet. Or the family in *Fiddler on the Roof*. Or any of the characters inside *West Side Story*.

When we marry outside of our tradition, we marry a journey to find the other. We don't really know the other yet because we don't know their tradition the way we know our tradition. Of course, you can both be Democrats, and both make seventy-two thousand a year or have a trust fund, and *still* embark on a journey. Marriage is almost always an adventure, a series of surprises, something that curious people enjoy. Just because you have modified the variables for success in your favor does not mean that you won't separate or divorce or end up in a marriage counselor's office.

My first husband was Lutheran, like me. We were both from working-class immigrant German families. We were the first in our families to go to college. We knew each other's traditions. We divorced. My husband now is Jewish, upper class, and we have lived happily together for almost forty years. By happy, I mean happy most of the time. I am a Christian pastor, and we raised our children in Sunday school at my church and then in Hebrew school at his synagogue. Two of our three children identify and practice as Jews; the third is remarkably postsecular, the definition of which is to come. My eldest son married a rabbi. He wears a personally designed T-shirt around Brooklyn (where else) that says, "My mother is a minister; my wife is a rabbi; get over it."

Postsecular means a new field, out beyond spiritual but not religious. Religious went first. Then the "nones" came along. Then spirituality engaged the "nones" and a few decided to be "spiritual but not religious." Now people are so far away from reactivity against punishmental religion or religion enforced by parents that they make spiritual pursuit a very minor one in their lives. Maybe Christmas? Maybe Easter? Maybe Rosh Hashanah? Every other year? If we have time?

They are acquainted with "spirituality" and have a sincere reach for transcendence, as long as few institutions are attached to it. "I don't like institutional religion" is a near cliché. I often quip that people should come to my congregation as we are significantly disorganized. These people don't get the joke. They would feel evil walking into a church. Churches have self-polluted and are perceived by the oft-used word "churchy." Say "church" and people feel judged. They wonder what they have done wrong. If I tell someone at a cocktail party that I am a clergyperson, the first thing I hear next is "What did I say?" Say "clergy," people feel judged. The truth is I am in the business of forgiveness and grace, not punishmentalism.

Postsecularists may also be fed up with the selfishness of secularism and are experimenting anew. New religious practices join new spiritual practices, like meditation or yoga, in popping up everywhere. Sociologists call this new field "postsecular." You are neither for nor against religion or spirit. If anything, after three generations have passed, you have no idea what religion is or was. You are spiritually unprepared, emptied as it were, of the past, so much so that you are ready for something new that you yourself design and practice. Individualism is the basis, pragmatism its pal. We belong to these two values more than to any other values. They undergird us. They bind us. They relativize each other constantly. "Whatever works." "Personal meaning." They hold us together. If one partner is not happy and finds another, even inside marriage, they did what they individually had to do. We understand. We may not be happy about it, but we "get it." Postsecularism understands that we are at a new threshold. That's why this book is a guide to transition, not complete trends or new cultural institutions. It's about what we do in the middle time, as pioneers, as newcomers to Spirit and Spirit's direction.

Often, I will meet with an engaged couple, and they will say they want a "church" service, but could I please not mention God. I call this the "no mention of God" moment. I will smile and say, "Sorry, no can do." They will wince, having been advised by some referral that I wasn't stuffy or churchy. I respect their caveat fully. God has been polluted for them. They want above all, like many in the "nones" or "none of the above" camp, to not be insincere during their marriage ceremony. They don't want to lie about God. They want to be sincere about not knowing God or liking God or needing God. They want a little truth in their very important moment, not even a hint of a lie or compromise. I understand.

We may end up not using any God language in their service, but first I will introduce my best friend, sometimes called God, other times called breath or force or energy, always that which is larger than me.

I will tell them how important God is to me. I first met the one whose name is more than Jesus, or Allah, or Christ, or breath, or force or even God as a child. My parents had a really rough marriage, so rough that my father frequently beat my mother up. (They were both German immigrants and Christian raised.) One night, when I was around six, the fighting started. I called the pastor at the Lutheran church up the street. He came, wearing his black cassock. He didn't stop the fighting forever, but he stopped it for then. And he made me and my siblings feel safe, secure, surrounded by a responsible adult. I dedicated my life that night to keeping little girls safe. I also started baptizing my dolls and giving them communion. My grandparents thought it was "cute" and assured me that women couldn't be pastors. They were wrong.

Anyway, in these no mention of God moments, I might also use a scripture, like the one from Romans 8. It still astonishes me how few people know anything of the ancient texts. I wouldn't know how to live without them. Yes, I have a cultural improficiency here. Romans 8:39 says, "[Nothing can] separate us from the love of God." Not agnosticism or unbelief, or neutral unbelief, or even suffering. If the couple thinks they will never suffer, they have another thing coming.

St. Paul's letter to the people at Rome argues that God's love conquers all. He knows that the power of suffering is enormous. And then argues that the power of God is ginormous. Suffering: 10; Love: 11. There is something larger than even the most beautiful partnership. You will need something larger than even the most beautiful partnership, if for no other reason than the following. One of you will predecease the other. Then what do you do? On what do you depend? Many men die quickly after their wife dies. That's why it is so good that most women do not predecease their husbands.

Buddhists say similar things differently. When we suffer, uninvited visitors knock on our door. We can either let them in or refuse to answer or invite them in for what Pema Chodron calls a "to go" cup of coffee or tea. We can say yes, you may enter but you can't stay. You can say I can't control what happened to me or to my child or my lover—but I can control my responses. Elie Wiesel argued exactly this about the Holocaust: I can't change what happened, but I can change how I see what happened. You don't get to take over my house. This is my house. Viktor Frankl came to a similar conclusion. Many who "get acquainted with grief" come up with very similar answers: we have the freedom to respond to suffering. It doesn't just "happen." It is tutored in us, often by religious observance.

Spiritually prepared people know how to pick themselves up when even the love of their life disappears. They have resilience. They live large lives, ones that help them love their intimates very, very deeply but not idolatrize them. By idolatrize, I mean not confusing anything small with God, even if the so-called small is the most important promise and partner of your life.

Lots of people have patterns to manage suffering. Suffering has at least three psychological responses. One is flight; the second is fight; the third is freeze. Flight is avoidance, even though the knock on the door puts on the costume of constant worry or fret. Fighting may work for a while, but some realities can't be conquered. Freezing, if a choice, is good for a while. If it becomes our new normal, we lose our ability to feel anything whatsoever while icing the suffering.

These are patterns that are very important, and they do work to manage suffering. Practicing the presence of Spirit in our lives is less a technology than it is a habit. We mention God not with any certainty but instead with longing and hope. God is much too large for any one culture's naming or theology or scriptures. Much too large. Oddly, the new physics has made the notion of God much more plausible. God wasn't just creating the human but the universe. Why? Some theologians that I love who are very pagan (a positive word to me) argue that God made the universe for the bubbles. I like that idea.

I also like St. Paul when he says that nothing can separate us from the love of God. We don't need to separate from God's goodness while suffering. Not all suffering comes around death. But death has the lead in the play of suffering.

Suffering can walk in off the street any time it wants. When you sign up and promise out loud and in public that you will love someone forever or till death do you part, you are also signing up to the suffering. The joy, yes, and the suffering, yes. Sickness, health. Richer, poorer. For better, for worse. You are signing up to maximize the other's joy, the other's power, the other's agency, the other's vocation. And you are signing up to accompany the suffering as well.

I have been doing some work with Alec Baldwin, who helped us start a series in my church on the North Fork. We called the first session "Spirituality in the Light of Covid." Alec talked about his own early failed marriage and nearly lost daughter as his first significant suffering. Someone whom he would not call God, because the word is so polluted and overused, showed up for him. He thinks COVID-19 is a dress rehearsal for the climate emergency, and I agree. Suffering is not a possibility; it is a probability. And then the gun! Who could have predicted that? Wouldn't anyone need "spirituality" or light or both? Spiritual preparation can make horrible things a little less horrible.

Our American innocence about suffering shows up in the way we don't prepare for things. Suffering shows up, surreptitiously, in drug use, addiction, and the enormous amounts of things and calories we seem to need to have around us. Neither pragmatism nor individualism prepares you for how empty life can be without genuine security. Security—be safe, as we like to say when we leave each other for the day—comes from the Hebrew word "shalom," the Christian word "salvation." It means safety, the deep kind. The one that doesn't get bowled over when all the pins get knocked down. The one that Pastor Witte gave me that night when he showed up. He didn't stop the hitting but he showed up.

Addiction is often understood as a flawed reach for transcendence or a narrative deficit disorder or just a need to get above it all. If you've ever said at night when you go to watch a lot of dumb TV, "I just want to chill or vegetate," you get it. Life can be too much even without COVID-19 or even without spousal abuse or even without addiction.

I will mention God to couples because I will mention suffering and its inevitability. When you partner, you promise to stick together through joy and suffering. You will need a family, friends, and a familiar. You might admit to those needs. You may or may not admit to needing God.

Imagine being John the Baptist's mother. She couldn't have known that he would be beheaded. But she knew he had made commitments that were troubling to the powers that be. Imagine, alternatively, what it would be like to be the mother of a real twenty-five-year-old who overdosed and died, right after spending two great weeks with his family and assuring them all that he was drug-free. Or being my daughter when her two-year-old said she had eaten a water bead, the kind that expands to forty times its size once placed in water inside a balloon. It is fun to watch the balloon pop. It is not fun to imagine that your child has eaten one and is about to explode.

My granddaughter had not eaten the water bead, but that was only proven after five hours in the emergency room, trying to decide about surgery, since water beads are translucent and don't necessarily come up on an X-ray. We found the water beads, both of them, on the floor after returning from the emergency room. You can sign the petition against this children's game online. Or join my Jewish daughter in saying Jesus Crisis.

When the water bead incident happened in my kitchen, while they were with us for the second long stay during COVID-19, I knew to step back and let the two mothers handle it. I just stood by. What I witnessed for the long distress was how much they supported each other. No one started shouting or blaming. Each of them dove deep for spiritual resources to keep them and the two-year-old calm. No one needed to mention God either. They were safe in themselves and with each other. It was a beautiful way to watch my Jewish daughter and her Mexican American Catholic wife interact.

Parents never know what is going to happen to their children. John the Baptist was beheaded, likely long after Elizabeth was gone. Or we certainly hope so. Most people have children when they marry. Children are never easy. Never.

Before the one called the Baptizer died an awful death, he "invented" baptism, a super-soaker ceremony if there ever was one. A water bead of a kind, capable of great magnification. Just water, we say. But then again, is there any water that is just water? My kids did not baptize my granddaughter. They gave her a naming ceremony, using Jewish ritual. More importantly, they super-soaked her with their calm and love, even when they were terrified that they had permitted something absurd to happen that might have hurt her.

Albert Einstein is said to have said that there are two kinds of people, those who don't believe in miracles and those who think everything is a miracle. Mothers have to believe everything is a miracle. Why? Because like Mary and Elizabeth, they have given birth. Joseph understood parenting just as well. He got the memo about Herod on his way "home."

Imagine loving your child, your partner, your life and still knowing what a stupid accident is when your two-year-old fishes out toys from a box her five-year-old cousin's father had sent over.

Scripture also tells us that "Herod [would] seek the child to destroy him" right after the baby was born and Christmas Eve's tenderness was over. Mary and Joseph had to return home another way because Herod was after their baby. Thank God for their dreams.

The best book I have read in a very long time is by Ta-Nehisi Coates, *The Water Dancer*. It is a story about the Underground Railroad, about dreams, about flight and how Herod doesn't win. Hiram tells a long story of losing his mother as she tries to escape slavery. He becomes the aid to "Moses." They are always going home another way, tricking their wannabe masters repeatedly. They even "swim" across the Delaware River at Philadelphia. They follow a great conduction, conducting something like the Grail in Dan Brown's great story. Their path becomes clear after they take their steps, not before. They do not experience a Jesus crisis. They experience what Jesus experienced as a baby. Protection by way of dream and dreaming!

Perhaps you have had a dream that tells you to change course. To conduct change. To go underground. To split. To cover your tracks. To take another way. I sure have, repeatedly.

Something, like God, the one who doesn't care whether you mention a name or not, will protect you whether you do something stupid or have to be questioned by the authorities or are a famous actor who is just trying to love his wife and children and has a second chance to do so. Religion and marriage may be changing, but suffering intends to persist. You will need to be spiritually prepared. You will want to be mutually powerful for each other. Both are possibilities. Both a strong healthy partnership and some spiritual preparation will help you squeeze the joy out of life and not get destroyed by the suffering.

QUESTIONS TO PONDER

1. If you fall in love with someone outside your tradition, race, class, religion, you could stop dating right away out of a sense of principle. You might want to preserve Jewish people. You might not want the hassle of learning a new culture or having a disapproving in-law. Or you could "just" date and become friends and help each other find a same-tradition partner. How will you ever know if you've done the right thing?

2. Imagine the worst thing that has ever happened to you—an ingested water bead or some other substance that might cause you to die or explode. What really helped? How did you get through it?
3. Who is Herod in your dreams? Is it your boss or parents or an abuser or bully of some kind? How do you figure out how to get home another way?
4. What is safety to you? What is spiritual safety to you?
5. What makes you secure? Do you have any false gods floating around? Do they help?

2

Why Marry at All?

WHY DO PEOPLE MARRY IN THE FIRST PLACE? THE PRIMARY REA-son is that we used to marry to have children. It was, second-arily and simultaneously, also a rite of passage into adulthood. You moved out of your parents' home into your own home. More hidden and nonetheless more real, marriage was a kind of insur-ance policy. Charlotte Perkins Gilman, author of *The Yellow Wall-paper*, argues that women married for different reasons than men. We married, she says, for insurance. Back when we couldn't make our own livings, outside the work we did at home, we needed a man for our salary. Louisa May Alcott agreed: She is said to have stated, "marriage costs the loss of half your freedom and doubles your obligations." The battle over gay marriage showed just how many hidden benefits marriage had—in insurances, cohousing, social status, help with housework, and more.

People used to marry because everybody else did and it was a ticket to social acceptance and acceptability. If you didn't marry, people wondered why.

Even earlier than these modern answers to the question of why, there was a biological pattern. Call it Noah's ark or two by two or whatever you want: people married to protect the intimacy that leads to children. Sexual urges developed rather normally and nicely around the same time that human beings could reproduce biologically. Religion and culture put sex in a neighborhood called "after marriage." Likewise, virginity had rules attached to it. Before marriage, you were a virgin. A girl. A boy. After marriage, you were a woman or a man. Along came birth control and put recreation into procreation. People used to have lots more children because they needed to ensure their own tradition's survival—and also they needed help on the farm. The originally cultural, then religious coupling carried meaning for the two people who so committed. The protection of sex from procreation added insurance policies, rites of passage, and children all in one nice package.

Arranged marriages predated unarranged individually chosen marriages. The definite trend in premodern and now postmodern worlds is to have fewer rules attached to marriage. (Some say that dating sites are a digital form of arranged marriages, and they are a big change, as previously mentioned, in how marriage "starts.") The state still gets involved eventually, but no longer does a couple receive disapproval from family if they "live together" before or after marriage or if they bring their families together after they divorce. Stepping is normal. Stepchildren are normal. Blended families are normal.

Let's take each of these in turn. First, we marry to have children. Today a man or a woman or a same-sex couple can adopt a child, with or without benefit of marriage. Marriage still helps with the adoption process but is not required. Anthropologist Margaret Mead often encouraged a two-stage marriage, back in the early part of the twentieth century. First you live together; then you marry when you are ready to add children. Her advocacy has pretty much been adopted. It is the rare couple that hasn't already had sex, lived together, shared a rental if not a mortgage. We practice marriage before we commit in public to it or go off the pill or take out the diaphragm or take off the condom.

Having children is more a biological event than a cultural or religious event, but obviously culture and religion have risen all around it to protect it. We add romantic love to the act of marriage today, but you could also imagine partnerships of people that were "just" designed to protect the children. Many people coparent to disallow the rules of marriage in having an effect—and they get all the benefits of the insurance policy without the fuzzy assumptions about forever or whatever.

When people marry, they pass into adulthood. We even have words for this today. Rites of passage or adulting. Adulting is when we move out of our parents' home into our own home. Or get a driver's license so we can move around independently. Or buy a house. Or get a college or high school degree. Adulting is also part of the ritual of marriage. We literally walk away from our parents (used to be our father giving us away) and walk toward our new first squeeze. In a ritual, you enter as one person, and you leave as another. In marriage, you become an adult, like in no other way, save perhaps when the first child is born. Then you adult even more when the first grandchild is born. Or your partner dies, and you become a widow or widower.

Change is constant. Evolution is constant. No one ever stays in the same stage of life for long. That is why rituals are important at every stage and why the marriage ritual is particularly important. As a pastor, I call my work hatching, matching, dispatching. Baptizing, marrying, burying. And more and more people understand the importance of intermediate rituals. At a miscarriage. Or a divorce. Or the first skin cancer.

If anything, recent events like the Covidation and secularization of life have stripped us of adulting rituals. Baptisms occur later and later. Bar and Bat Mitzvahs become more individualized and people "permit" the nonparticipation of the rabbi or the participation of what we call custom-designed services. All the hatchings, matchings, and dispatchings are on hold. My niece just canceled her wedding for the third time.

The more recent the immigrant, the more likely they are to have services that "adult" preteens and bind them to their past. As immigrant families become third- and fourth-generation families, they go the way of all earlier immigrants. They become less bound to their past and more bound to their present and what they imagine to be their mixed futures. So, yes, marriage is a rite of passage into adulthood. The decrease in attention paid to the rituals of marriage may mean there are fewer adults or that we individually are less adult. That is a matter that deserves serious consideration. Did we just change the meaning of the word "adult" or did we get less prepared to grow up? I think the latter. I think we need culture, religion, and "folk" thinking to become an adult. I think individualism offers false promises of any sense of belonging to anyone—and robs us of much beauty in life. I also think we need patterns to adult well. And things that used to be called morals, which today I would call guidance, direction, focus, boundaries. What *is* right or wrong about divorce? How do we know? Adults know how to keep promises longer and better, in my experience. Half adults or unformed adults or lost adults barely know how to belong to themselves, much less a life partner, much less a child. (The moving back in with parents during COVID-19 showed a lot of us how we belonged to each other—both parent and adult child—and it also showed us how much we prefer to be on our own.)

David Brooks has written a lot about the nuclear family and its failures to prepare us for adult futures. He tells us that 27 percent of American families have a stranded person in them. By stranded we mean one grown child or one parent or one grandparent or one sibling is just abandoned. We no longer connect to them because they "don't meet our needs."[1] Brooks also had a significant piece in the *Atlantic* in March 2020, arguing that the nuclear family has been a mistake.[2]

Some of the reasons for the nuclear family's problems in maturing us have to do with the reduction of the grounds for marriage to sociological ones. The glue isn't there without the support of religion. For children, for insurance, for rites of passage—these are all good reasons to marry. But they don't hold you long enough to deal with the difficulties of being married or to be prepared for its joys. They are tough seeds to plant in shallow, rocky, or sandy ground. The human is built to belong, to bind, to secure self and others—and likes to think of these matters as sacred as well as secular. When the sacred dissolves, the seed doesn't grow into its great mystery or flowering. To summarize Brooks's much more complex argument, just think about marriages you know or even your own. People marry later. They divorce more. They think in "ideal" terms of 2.5 kids, one a boy, the other a girl, the other a statistic. Christopher Lasch, American historian, argues that marriage didn't just "fall apart." It had been falling apart for over a hundred years, as advanced secularism, materialism, individualism, and pragmatism moved in on religion and took its place.

I am not one bit surprised at this analysis nor in dispute with it. Religion self-polluted and became exactly what Jesus and many other prophets came in to turn over. Religion, and, yes, I am religious, from cradle and likely to my grave, became captive to its own inner darkness. Some Catholic bishops today contemplate denying the Eucharist to President Biden because of his stand on abortion. When the Eucharist is denied to a sinner (as the bishops see it), they have destroyed the Eucharist. The Eucharist is *for* sinners, not against them/us. When congregations think of their clergy as privately owned chaplains, they are already unreligious.

I don't even want to mention boring sermons or churches that have their noses way too high in the air or sexual abuse by priests. Many talk about the Crusades as being their "evidence" against religion. They could find much evidence in more recent times. Spiritual injury and moral injury are real, quite evidently.

The mess religious institutions have made of themselves is real, palpable. It is our own "fault" that lesser gods took up our space. Brooks sees this problem and at least acknowledges it out loud. He is religious enough to imagine that we made a mistake. He points to many repentant and interesting developments.

The modern chosen family movement is one. Coparenting without benefit of marriage, like well-considered roommates, is another. Intergenerational living experiments are increasing again, thanks likely to COVID-19. They may or may not be in blood families. The real estate industry reports that a whopping 44 percent of people search first for a home that has an in-law or extra apartment or living space, so that generations can coinhabit. Multigenerational buildings or two generations comfortably under one roof are popping up everywhere.

Sociologist Eli Finkel says that the kinds of marriages we have now are fundamentally "self-expressive" and designed not so much for even children but for the adults' self-fulfillment.

This reductionism about the sacrament of marriage is the genuine problem. A good reason to marry is that it is holy to do so. Not easy. Not required. But chosen, as a route to holiness.

When people say marriage is also an insurance policy, which is not the nicest thing to say about it, they debase the sacred vows of promise and commitment, the adult vows of thick and thin, richer, poorer, sickness, health, better, worse. We feel the cynicism when people say marriage is "just" an insurance policy. We could say instead that insurance policies are great things and that we wish everyone had one. The promise to take care of one another through thick and thin is an awesome thing. A truly awesome thing. That sense of security that you won't die alone is a holy one.

Marriage can be seen through some people's sacramental attachment to our pets. We find ourselves very spiritual when our cat dies. We know it's silly, but we bother to analyze it too much. Many of us "put down" a cat and never remember that we might have to "put down" a beloved mother, father, wife, or husband.

Marriage has changed because people have become more cynical about it. They/we think it is about money or status or biology or sex, but it's actually about shalom, security, salvation, being safe, all of which are beautiful religious promises from the creator. Marriage is about having and giving so much security to another that you live powerfully and freely. You are in charge, not not in charge. You don't have to be like me and believe and trust in God to enjoy security. But you might want the experience of the holy.

When we marry, we imitate the unconditional love God has for us. We don't succeed in loving unconditionally but we point and aim in that direction.

I have never understood why people think sex debases romance so much or why people need the fantasy of "falling in love" so much. Why? It is obvious, at least to me, that marriage is a form of blessed, much-needed, delightful security. That is why people marry. The ancillary benefits are also delightful.

Married couples pay fewer taxes, live longer, have more economic security, and don't always have to do all the dishes all the time. The increase in women's freedom to be self-supporting has changed some of the energy of Charlotte Perkins Gilman's slam at the infantilization of marriage as an insurance policy. But it is still true that marriage is an economic advantage, even if for no other reason than it pays the rent. Two is better than one. When I say that marriage is holy and is a pursuit of the holy, I am not demeaning these great reasons to marry. I am just adding some bubbles to them.

As a card-carrying feminist, I have long rued the way the economy changed just as women entered the workforce more fully. We have always worked. Housework, vegetable growing, and raising children are all work. Duh. Ask anyone who is in a family with two full-time jobs what they pay for childcare or house cleaning. But that brief period in the 1950s when women were "allowed" to stay home was a unique economic period. Two salaries are very much needed if not required today to establish a middle-class life. It would be wonderful if everyone could work part-time and everyone could take care of children and cook food and enjoy the blessing of a cleaned-up home! The economy is simply not structured for that at this point. Thus, the two-career family predates most consideration of developing the joy of cultural proficiency. Here I am establishing what marriage is for most couples, whether they are mixed or not.

Almost no one lives in a clean or clear home today. Dining rooms are going extinct. Kitchen counters are the hearth.

Even architecture and "housekeeping" recognize how much things have changed in the cynical insurance policy direction as a definition of marriage. When people say, "My house is a mess," usually they are not kidding. The sneaky, unintentional undermining of marriage is the reason houses are a mess. We aren't having enough fun with our security. We are pretty convinced by individualism that we are not secure because why would anybody bother taking care of anyone else. Or making a home for them.

Why do I dislike the flattening of secularism so much? Or dislike its individualism so much? Because it hurts people and doesn't help people. It makes us sour, lonely, and longing. It promises independence that causes people to be afraid of each other.

These sociological factors regarding marriage really matter as the bedrock for all kinds of marriages, within your own tradition and outside your own tradition. You marry to have children, you marry for the insurance policy, and you marry to become an adult.

There are also a lot of subliminal reasons to marry, in or outside your tradition. You marry because your parents had a good relationship, and you didn't even know that was why you wanted to marry. You may or may not know in your head that you want children, but you may be surprised, as I was at thirty-eight, when a biological time bomb goes off in your womb or your penis. You marry because you want to ensure your tradition's future. You marry because your economic systems are built on partnership. You marry because you understand the value of rites of passage, because you are almost biologically driven to become a spouse. You marry because you want security. You want to "settle down." I will say more about that unfortunate language later. Again, all these reasons have an ounce of the holy and the common and the psychological and sociological to them. They are great reasons. They are rarely enough to make for a good marriage.

The Other Reasons

It's probably already clear that I think marriage could be understood as a blessing rather than a sociological necessity. We could love it rather than just "do it." We could resacralize it rather than just "do" it or "succeed" at it.

Less sociological reasons to marry go straight back to the heart of religion. As mentioned previously, religion comes from the word *religare* and means "to bind." In marriage, we bind ourselves and our money and our families and our sexuality to each other. We find ourselves belonging to each other. We *belong*. We get all twisted up—as anyone who has ever had a divorce will tell you. Your name. Your address. Your bank accounts. All are bound up together and very hard to "separate" much less divorce.

When I divorced, as a woman who had married too young and made the mistake of choosing his very calm family of origin (relatively) compared to my turbulent one, I had to fight to keep his name. Why? I had written three books and I wanted the name. I had also married him for his mother, an ideal mother for me at that stage in my life. We are still connected. My ex and I collaborated in making case law in Connecticut. He wanted the name back. I didn't want to be the Rev. Donna Osterhoudt and lose book sales. Of course, they were not the real reasons, but how did we know as we unbound to each other and went on the "rebound"? I won the name. I will speak later in the book a lot about how good marriages result from good balances of power and bad marriages result from bad balances of power. Artful balancing of personal power with independence and dependence is one good definition of marriage. Many individualistic people even like it as a definition.

In this case, I "won," got the power. I also became heartbroken because I had broken a promise. Winning can also be losing. The distress I experienced for two years after we finally divorced was an indication of how holy our belonging was in the first place.

In my current marriage, I kept my name because becoming the Rev. Dr. Donna Goldstein was going to cause nothing but trouble. Even at the seemingly simple level of our names, we bind together. And we also bind hearts and rarely know how much, even in divorce.

Theologians often say that religion binds us "back" as well. By back they mean to our origins, our ancestry, our parents, their traditions, what they said to each other on whatever boat brought them to the United States. Or elsewhere. Binding back is that high regard we all have for tradition, whether we know it or not. Rebellion against a tradition is as much connection to it as not. We may even find ourselves in a reactive position. When we say anything about any past, whether positive or negative, we are re-acting. The past has power. We are rarely, if ever, acting. We are shaped by our pasts, by blood, by our names, by our associations. Associations are that strange combination of culture and religion that tells us what days we take off for Sabbath and when we work, or what to wear, or what to eat. Culture shows up in cuisine and in halal and how to cook the rice. As we mature, we realize that other people are as bound to their traditions as we are to ours. That is what we call cultural proficiency, the capacity to appreciate our culture without absolutizing it, the capacity to understand that there are many cultures in the world God made. Maturity often develops into generativity and generosity: we don't just understand diversity, we appreciate diversity.

In the United Church of Christ, my home denomination, despite my origin in the tradition of Lutheranism, we have some code language for congregations where GLBTQ people are likely to be at home. The code is ONA or Open and Affirming. Using this code to let people know who was welcome and who wasn't in a congregation, everybody said they were open. Almost no one said that GLBTQ people would be unwelcomed. The word "affirming" got people into a first-class toot.

Isn't being gay a sin? Isn't being trans a sin? No, they are not. But many people, even today, still think so. How can you affirm a sin? Well, you can't affirm a sin, but loving same-gendered or fluidly gendered people is not a sin. How to make the motion from maturity to generativity? It is by learning how to appreciate diversity, enjoy it, be amused by it, be interested in it. You may need to take a dose of religion also. You may need to dive deep to find out why you are just open and not affirming of diversity.

If you marry outside your tradition, you will maximize your chances for marital happiness by enjoying the diversity of your partner. "Toleration" will take you through a year or two. Appreciation will help the love last. Religion is not perfect, but it is helpful to generativity, maturity, and the capacity to appreciate, both self and other.

QUESTIONS TO PONDER

1. What is marriage to you? Is it a thing or more than a thing? In what ways is it holy? In what ways is it practical? Can it be both?
2. If you married and couldn't have children for some reason, what would you do? Would you adopt? Or care for your nieces and nephews instead? Would you feel like a failure? How would you cope?
3. What is a religious reason to marry? Do you like the idea of doing something holy and hard? Can you be both a traditionalist and a seeker?
4. What were your vows when you married, if you married? Or what were your parents' vows? What did they promise out loud to each other?
5. How does the state get involved with the sociological—all good stuff—and the spiritual—all good stuff? How can we change our binary thinking about marriage? What if it is both economic and practical and spiritual at the same time?

3

Habits, Culture, and Prayer

MARRIAGE IS STILL FUNDAMENTALLY ABOUT INTIMATE BELONG-ing. It is secondarily or next about belonging outside your tradition of origin. Marriage is marriage whether inside or outside your origins. It may even be about making a new kind of tradition or belonging, whether consciously or not. So far in human biological history, there is no such thing. Traditions are sequences of ancestors who share genetic and cultural material. When you add a new genome to a tradition, it changes the tradition biologically and then changes the tradition culturally as well. Of course, we are a bit "confused" about how to handle new genomic material, new cultural material—and this confusion comes back to adapt marriages. When you marry outside your tradition, these matters of genomic shift and cultural shift *will* show up in your bedroom and at your kitchen table, whether you invite them or not. That's why I advocate so fiercely for spiritual preparation.

Your partner may be Jewish and get depressed right before Rosh Hashanah every year and not even know why. If you fail to get your Christian partner an Easter basket, she may be miffed, while feeling immature about being so. If your Muslim partner is invited to a dinner party with you and pork is the main event on the menu, sparks may fly all the way home. The more conscious we can be about each other—and how a mother is to be treated, if you are Italian and she is Polish—the better. Consciousness joins awareness in being the prelude to spirituality.

Many famous people have changed their ancestral trajectory by marrying outside their tradition. I read and follow Marian Edelman, an African American Baptist woman who married a white Jewish man and raised children in both traditions. I read and follow Shelby Foote, a Southern Baptist who married a Jew in New Orleans and lived to tell some great stories. Or C. S. Lewis, the famous Christian writer who married, late in life, a Jewish woman who had converted to Christianity. He then assured one of her children a Jewish education after she died. These educated and accomplished people are wedge figures; they represent the inevitable blending of the population as cultural markers themselves.

As part of the new and ongoing revelation of God, these people are showing us something important, if expansive and if dilute. What they are showing is not *just* biological, although it begins biologically in the change of the lineage. They are developing new blended pieties. Pieties are ways to practice the presence of God. They are a fancy word for prayer. They are habits. Routine maintenance is something we do for our cars; we also need to take care of our spirits habitually.

Habits are the thing that culture yields. Of course, we always have breakfast at the table in the morning at eight. Doesn't everyone? Habits can be very important parts of religious observance. They cohere our Sundays or Saturdays. They help us wake in the morning and go to sleep at night.

I wake in the morning praying because I was taught by my German family that praying was the way you wake up. I go to sleep at night praying for the same reason. In the morning, I quote a famous Protestant theologian: "The purpose of life is to praise God and enjoy God forever." Amen. Do it today, Donna. At night I rest in thanking God for my partner, my children, my grandchildren and switch the order because I usually fall right asleep. Sometimes I just pick one of them and visualize and love their face.

The Koran advises, "Rest and Remembrance." It also says, "Rarely without the remembrance of God does the heart find peace." This Koranic material sounds German to me but that's because I start with my grandparents' advice. My Muslim student, Faith, who lives alone tells me that he also remembers his three rabbits, Raja, Quinn, and Truffle, as he falls asleep. His family is all dead; he is twenty-eight. He rests with his rabbits. Prayer doesn't have to be heavy laden; it can be light of spirit as well. Piety has the sound of heaviness, but it need not be so. Ask the Dolly Mama, which is my pen name and to whom you will be introduced later.

Piety is the habit of prayer in everyday life. It is a devotion to religious duties and practices. It comes as a word from a German movement founded by P. J. Spener (1635–1705), who advocated a revival of the devotional idea in the Lutheran Church. Today we hear the word "spirituality" used interchangeably with the more old-fashioned "piety." "I am developing my spirituality" translates quite well to mean I am devoting myself to religious duties and practices. Or I am devoting myself to developing and disciplining my piety, my practice of the presence of God.

The people who create their own inner, private, sacred space are often doing so in response to a perceived institutional abuse of piety, where people faked religious affection by hollow observances. This very lack of trust in the old wineskin has resulted in a devotional flowering among individuals. Meditation is absolutely a beautiful and ancient form of prayer and devotion. Spiritual habits needed a new word.

Again, the loss of the old sacred spaces has opened and expanded the place of the sacred in the lives of people. There is more, not less, God in normal lives. People read devotions and read them devotionally; they walk labyrinths; they fast and pray. They use therapeutic interventions to stop the constant self-reproach that culturelessness permits. People meditate and do physical practices like yoga and tai chi devotionally. There is a new piety, and it is growing. At New York University, three out of five students have a meditation practice; two out of five enjoy a physically spiritual observance like yoga or tai chi. The chaplaincy program there encourages these practices as ways to relax uptight students. We might speak religiously: students who are anxious are searching for peace. The devil is fear; the god is peace. These are culturally approved practices of piety, or prayer, or meditation, or pause. They also sit on the edge of many of our traditions of origin, a place of comfort for those of us uncomfortable with some of the spiritual ways in which we were raised.

These people are developing new cultures, all based on the new biologies. Some, like me, find this very exciting; others are afraid of it. Here I affirm and enjoy it. And I recommend such openness to habitual piety to people who marry each other, whether inside or outside their tradition of origin.

Consider these enormous shifts as metaphors that involve change and the art of changing. They show how belonging changes as we change the ways we belong. Students meditate or do yoga because other students do. They are making culture together. In intimate relationships we need culture even more than we do in friendships. Consider these few stories.

My friend lives in a house on a hill in western Massachusetts that was built in 1850. She loves it and bought it the moment she saw the mountains down the hill, to the meadow to the Connecticut River to the mountains on the next ridge over. She is an expert on the French postmodern theorist Derrida and taught in California for most of her life. In other words, she is a bit of a nomad, definitely an intellectual; she was born in Vermont on a place that looked a lot like this one, her retirement home. The house is in marvelous shape except that it is sinking a bit. Wide pine boards join long windows that capture the hills on all sides. They don't call western Massachusetts the Hilltowns for nothing.

The problem is in the foundation of the house. Its joists need to be sistered. When she first said she had found someone who could sister the joists, I thought she was making a good joke. She wasn't. She was talking about repairing the foundation, which can be done in one of two ways. You can put another beam next to the beam that is holding up the house. Sistering A, let's call it. Or you can add a new kind of beam that is triangle shaped and wedges the foundation. Sistering B, let's call it. She is doing both. We had a few jokes at breakfast when she assured me that I wasn't in danger of falling through the kitchen floor. She "only" had to repair five of the fourteen joists. The house was on a firm, if eventually fragile, foundation. I made a sick joke about how that's what they said in Miami's Surfside Beach condo collapse too.

The need to bolster our foundations is clear to just about everybody—and some say we should redo the whole thing with new kinds of joists, which others say just repair.

Marriage is a beautiful old house that needs its foundations replaced *before* someone else falls through the difficulties of the new, for which so many of us are so fundamentally spiritually unprepared. Shall we carry on in a marriage that has lost its joy? Or are we free to leave it? Do we try propping it up with something just like the old prop, or do we use a new prop? How much do we love the old house and its new future? Enough to risk it falling in? Or enough to transform it into its next form of lineage?

I married a couple about ten years ago. (Officiated is what I mean.) They were both delightfully interesting people, she a food writer, he a chef. They had twins. They moved to the country. They divorced. She now has the four-year-old twins and is single parenting. He just walked. I spent easily ten premarital sessions with them when I usually only do six. Why? I sensed that the foundation was not strong in either of them. There was nothing wrong with either of them. They just had a lot of undigested suffering. She had lost her mother young and been ignored by her father. He was just too quiet about everything. They were both secular people whose religious origins (Catholic) had disappeared three generations ago. The new name for such well-educated, good-looking secular people is "postsecular." They are even postspiritual but not religious. She does a lot of yoga. He has a nearly spiritual relationship with food. They are fun to be with. And they needed a sistering of their joints several generations ago if this marriage was going to last. Or at least a new set of brackets side by side. They likely divorced because he thought of one way to spend his time off and she another. He thought he was right about the way to put children to bed and so did she. When the twins came, she wanted them baptized. He did not. They still agreed about food but not about much else. Both argued that they "didn't share the same values," even though these values showed up in commonplace discussions about commonplace things. The real issue was about power, not about bedtimes. Both felt they didn't have enough power, enough oomph, enough energy to "work it out." And they didn't because they hadn't stored enough maturity yet to manage to belong to each other. They didn't do anything *wrong*. What happened was that they didn't do enough *right* generations ago to prepare themselves culturally and spiritually to endure the rough spots of marriage and hard work. They also weren't having much fun. Spiritual confusion took the place of spiritual aliveness.

Take another story. I had a very hard relationship in college with sororities. I both really wanted to belong and really didn't want to belong. I avoided rush early and ended up sistering as a sophomore, de-sistering as a second-semester sophomore, re-sistering as a first-semester junior, and then de-sistering as a second-semester junior. (No wonder I loved my western Massachusetts friend's house.) Then I got married at the end of junior year and moved off campus. I just didn't have any idea where or how I wanted to belong to whom or what. And I wasn't an old house, just a young woman.

Religion means to bind. It involves joisting and joining and unjoining, belonging and unbelonging and much more. Spiritual preparation helps us feel good about the decisions we make at each turn in the road. Spiritual confusion breeds itself.

The fancy sociological language for these human patterns is affiliating, along with disaffiliating and reaffiliating. Sociologically, we see these three verbs as each part of the same action. More and more people are disaffiliating and not reaffiliating. It's almost like we are stuck in between the storms of old religions dying out and new ones being born. There we whirl—and still marry. Marriage is not for the immature or the unripened or unseasoned. It is for adults.

Woody Allen often joked that he didn't want "membership in any club that would have him." Notably, more and more people don't want to marry early because they know they are too young. The age of first marriages has increased to twenty-eight for women and thirty for men. It is at a historic high point. Thirty years ago the average age was twenty-two for men and twenty for women.

Rising interfaith marriages join rising ages for first marriages. Simultaneously, the growth of secularism is a trend, even as we have already said becoming a kind of postsecularism. The same biological matters are involved with shifts in biological ancestry becoming new progeny. Rarely does a very religious person or "traditional" person marry a very secular or cosmopolitan person. Marriage occurs in context of homogeneity, with like liking like. Yes, Republicans marry Republicans and Democrats marry Democrats. Many parents worry that some diversity might prevail in their in-laws and publicly express their discontent with that. With religious loss comes cultural loss. For the purposes of this book, I am talking about religious loss and its impact on marriage.

DISAFFILIATION AND ITS CONSEQUENCES

I had the privilege of working with a Catholic priest named Father Carl Chudy, who oversaw dealing with congregations that had emptied of young people. He was to study the enormous grief of grandparents who knew that their children no longer attended mass, not to even mention the children of their children. He talked to the real people and also studied the trends. He wrote an important doctoral dissertation titled "Intergenerational Issues & Religious Deconversion."

Religious deconversion or disaffiliation is a phenomenon that begins in the family, and is intergenerational in nature, with a history much longer than the coinage of the term "nones" in the early 1990s.[1] Despite the enduring American mythology of early settlement as motivated by Puritans' desire to practice religion freely, for many colonists "religious freedom," no matter that they would likely have seen themselves as at least nominally Christian, meant freedom from all religious dogmas and institutional demands, including the demand to claim a creed and attend worship regularly. That did not change dramatically until the mid-twentieth century.[2]

The landscape of American religion, despite the fears to the contrary, has been remarkably stable since the middle of the twentieth century, after World War II. Religiosity in families and individuals shows many going to religious services on a weekly basis, just like their grandparents did. Yet, Robert Putnam and David Campbell point to three successive aftershocks from the 1960s "whose seismographic records have gradually polarized the American religious scene," and, I would add, the American family.[3] They call the long, barely perceptible change over decades generational effect. An example of this slow, measured change is in adolescent religious observance over four decades, accelerating in the 1960s, 1990s, and early 2000s.[4]

They contend that the rate of change in American religion in the last forty years is faster paced. The first shock that represents this more rapid change was the shift from the 1950s' strong religious affiliation of one generation into a secular direction in the 1960s. The second aftershock, in reaction to the liberal direction, impelled a new generation into a conservative religious direction in the seventies and eighties. This sent yet another, third aftershock in the 1990s and early 2000s for a new generation in an even more pronounced nonreligious direction.[5]

This extraordinary arc of change was characterized from the unique upheavals of the 1960s of political and social assassinations, the setting of the stage of the culture wars, and changes in sexual mores. Thereby religious believers suffered losses in confidence, liberal and mainline Christians joined in social justice, the effects of Vatican II for Catholics changed traditional practice, and opposition to birth control ushered a dramatic decline in church attendance. Decline in religious observance fell to new lows.

Joel Thiessen and Sarah Wilkins-Laflamme state:

Among those who actively leave religion, we found that disaffiliation (1) is often a process, (2) sometimes involves multiple variables at work simultaneously, (3) is often linked back to a family context where each generation progressively became less religious and as a result religion was not that salient during one's upbringing (even if one was exposed to religious belief/ practice for a period of time), and (4) often comes to fruition when the individual becomes more independent from the original family household (when religion becomes seen as a choice, when intellectual disagreements arise with religion, when the individual enters into contact with less religious friends, and with life transitions). . . .

This does not mean that religious nones do not adopt various strands of religiosity or spirituality, though admittedly by most indicators they are far less religious than those who hold a religious affiliation and remaining personal religiosity and spirituality may further decline with each successive generation.[6]

The Public Religion Research Institute (PRRI) study *Exodus: Why Americans Are Leaving Religion—and Why They're Unlikely to Come Back* states "Roughly three in ten (31%) religious Americans who were brought up by divorced parents say they attend religious services at least once a week, compared to 43% of religious Americans who were raised by married parents."[7]

Interfaith marriages, or religiously mixed households, also play a role in disaffiliation. For example, among those who were raised Catholic, there is a strong correlation between those whose parents were both Catholic and those who had one parent with a different religious or nonreligious identity; about four in ten remain Catholic as adults. In contrast, almost two-thirds of those raised in Catholic households by parents who were both Catholic remain Catholic as adults. This carries over to the likelihood of religiously unaffiliated people to marry like-minded partners, about 54 percent. This is a shift from previous generations. Disaffiliation becomes intergenerational.

There are several matters important to my points here in the intergenerational process of disaffiliation. First is that there is some grief involved, for the grandparents, the parents, and the children. It is a different kind of grief but it is still a grief. It is an unremarked loss. It is a sadness that knows no name. When that happens, moral confusion results. Sometimes moral confusion becomes an absence of any kind of piety or a move into what are called "third spaces." These include therapy, yoga, meditation, affiliation with a seekers group, and many less institutional, more new age (in the best sense of that word) experiences. I often call moral confusion in the anything and everything goes experimental third spaces spiritual preparation for what is coming next. Of course, these are baby steps. Of course, they are wide open. They are *seeking*. They aren't like the old religions that are *found* places. They are moving between the storms. They are reaches. They don't have buildings, customs, vestments, orthodoxies. Often, they don't even have places and wander around. My daughter-in-law, a rabbi, formed the Beloved Community, a place for young Jews in Brooklyn to find each other and to explore religious practices and habits. At Hartford Seminary, where I teach, the Muslim students talk about the mantle of mercy, a new movement among young Muslims. Christians form "house churches."

Some of us still in the religious space, like me, call such people consumers. They come and go, they take and leave. Unfortunately, we religious types have some serious condescension in our tone. We also have grief. We feel abandoned and misunderstood, blah blah blah.

I often corrected my friends who made fun of those who say they are spiritual but not religious. I would say something like, "Isn't it great that people don't want to be phony or insincere about God? Don't you love the seeker seeking sincerely?" Sometimes my friends could hear me reaching for some resolution for our complex grief, other times not. Grief is a form of love. I do love religious institutions. They gave me life. And—not but—I am also still seeking sincerity in my piety about my relationship with God. I don't think I will ever stop. It also seems to me that it takes a whole life to even begin to become a Christian. And I have the benefit of a seminary education and much more lifelong learning and practice of my immature faith.

Moreover, I know that very few people even know Santayana, who will be quoted below. Or that French guy, Derrida. Or Mary Daly's book *Beyond God the Father*, which I read two pages every Tuesday night with a group of nuns when I was young enough to be shaped. Or Reinhold Niebuhr's two volumes *The Nature and Destiny of Man*. Just kidding, Mary Daly.

Santayana says, "We strive for a transcendental perspective devoid of any constrictions but we just glimpse the perspective of eternity. . . . Thus religion doesn't describe an otherworldly realm at all but this one idealized and represented mythopoetically." For Santayana, religion and even science are both kinds of poetry. He often indicts positivism as being unimaginative. I love critiques of religion as a religious person. Don't you?

Matters of belonging and binding are involved in religious observance, in seeking observance, in antireligious observance and prereligious observance. Religion won't "go away" for a long time. Our minds and our streets are littered with the evidence of its past presence. The question that matters is how the human belongs to God before belonging to a partner. There are belongings and there are Belongings. Spiritual maturity is a great help to those wanting to enjoy marriage and manage marriage. It comes from "getting right with God," or the ultimate or the energy or the force or the reason or the destination of the human *being*. When people partner with a sense of that question as primary and go on to respect each other's practice of the presence of that God,, marriage inside and outside the tradition becomes a blessing. It can also become a curse, absent such acknowledgments.

The Dolly Mama (whom you will get to know better later) would also say all this much more irreverently. She would likely say, "Why not have a primary relationship with an ultimate and a penultimate relationship with a penultimate? You like to play ultimate Frisbee, don't you? You know what's big and what's really big. Who does the laundry is not big. Which God you actually worship is Big. When the big meets the Big, you can likely get the laundry done with a lot less drama."

QUESTIONS TO PONDER

1. How do you pray if you pray? Would you like to pray?
2. How do you practice the presence of the most important thing in your life? What is practice to you? Is it a habit? Or an observance? Or a necessity?
3. How does your partner pray? Do you ever pray together? Why? Why not?

4

No Mention of God

WHEN WE MARRY, WHETHER INSIDE OR OUTSIDE OUR TRADITION, we complete one of the holiest of acts of our lifetime. We gather all our best friends and all our family. We dress up. We party. We eat together. We buy the best flowers we can afford. We pledge and promise. We say out loud that we will do impossible things. We do so "before God and this entire company," or at least we used to do so.

Now nine out of ten couples who come to ask me if I will officiate at their marriage make a shy request. They know enough to be embarrassed to ask, but still they ask, "Can you please not mention God?" I call this the "no mention of God moment."

I mightily appreciate the spiritual but not religious people for their sincerity. They don't want to lie about something as important as God. Nor do they want to embarrass any of their friends or family in public and make them sit through a prayer that doesn't ring true or a comment that makes them feel guilty for not having a "spiritual life." They know their crowd: secular, agnostic, perhaps even postsecular, that new phrase for the search for spiritual meaning that has overcome even the secularists.

Still, as a pastor, I want to bring God in some way, shape, or form into the promises that are being made. I want a blessing to occur. I want a covenant, not just a contract, to occur. I want to enlarge the space with a spirited presence. I want a three-hanky experience. I want a sense of transcendence. So do most couples. They just don't want anything judgy or embarrassing or insincere to also happen as God gets "mention."

You may not know Thumbtack, but it is a great place for clergy to advertise their "hatching, matching, and dispatching" skills. We get lots of requests and the majority of them carry the code "No mention of God."

My profile on Thumbtack says that I am a queer clergyperson, a renegade religionist, one who loves God and doesn't claim to be right in her interpretation of God.

I may not like religion, but I adore God. There is nothing more important to me than my relationship with the one I call God, not my husband or my children or my work. My denomination, the United Church of Christ, pioneered a slogan. "God Is Still Speaking" was our message to the concrete laid by literalists on the ancient texts. We were trying to pry religion open. We were trying to protect the scriptures from rigidity in interpretation. We wanted the word to become fresh and to dwell among us.

We never got on *Oprah* but we tried.

The Thumbtack consistency is the best evidence I know of how much my small town called the religious Left needs a new promotional campaign or at least a chamber of commerce. It shows how successful the religious Right has been in skewing religion to its most debased level. It also shows the extent of the moral injury done by organized religion. While trying way too hard to be right, religion has been on the wrong side of right. We queer and minority religious people lost God to the meanness and the rigidity and the fear—all things that good religion overcomes.

True confession: my side lost. Our ideas about God not only receive no mention, but our antagonists have been so wrong about God that they have taken God into the unmentionables. My side doesn't believe so much in winning and losing, so the offense is only taken at the chambered commercial level. God will be fine; God's people will not be. They will be spiritually homeless and starving and in profound need of a soup kitchen and a shelter.

Even National Public Radio reports that "most Christians" are judgy antigay grumps. The word "judgy" comes up first in the surveys about who Christians are, followed by "antigay."

We used to call my kind of argument here "apologetics." By that we meant we were apologizing for some of our representatives but not for the faith itself. My congregations have been mostly postdenominational and unapologetic about being Christians while knowing we have sneered way too often at way too many people. My last congregation was full of queers, misfits, atheists, agnostics, Jews, and at least one single woman and her child.

I tried to tell her she was too old to be a single parent. She was over forty. She had the child, and I was wrong. I'm still OK and she's still OK and we're OK and I was wrong. When I asked her who she thought would take care of the child if something happened to her, she said, "The church."

We called ourselves the perfect church for imperfect people or the best church you can't find, imitating the slogan of the Montague, Massachusetts, bookstore that says it is "books you don't need in a place you can't find."

When people ask me not to mention God, I think of this as a great opportunity to ask them which God I should not mention. I don't want to mention the judgy God or the literal God and I certainly don't want to do a lot of Jesus talk at an interfaith wedding of a Jew and a Christian. Nor vice versa.

There are five places where God can be mentioned in a marriage ceremony outside your tradition. These can be honest. Inclusive, modest, and open.

1. One is in the opening prayer. "God, you whom some call Allah, some call Jesus, others call Christ, others know as breath, still others call force or energy, You who are beyond the captivity of

any name, you of many names, draw near and bless the promises
about to be made. Amen." Why not?

2. Another is a land acknowledgment. "We are not the first peo-
ples on this land nor will we be the last. Help us to become good
ancestors and to represent the Spirit of this land and people as
well as we can."

3. When the vows are made, the officiant can explain that a vow is
a covenant as well as a contract, adding holiness and the sacred-
ness of intention to the legal promise.

4. The couple can also conclude their promises/vow by saying,
"With the help of God."

5. The ending: "Forasmuch as you, [name and name], have promised before God and this entire company, to be joined together
in a holy matrimony, I now pronounce you wife and wife [or
husband and wife or husband and husband]. What God has put
together let no one ever tear apart."

We may also add different godly meanings in funerals. Consider the use of "Ashes to ashes, stardust to stardust" instead of
"Ashes to ashes, dust to dust." We can shake up any service with
recollections of scripture or "movie" religious-type slogans.

When I did the memorial service for Gloria, a famous porn
star, whose movies I don't think I ever saw even though the packed
house of never-darken-the-door types had, I knew Gloria was
becoming a new kind of star. She was joining the aurora borealis,
which is what we all do. Hell is a projection of the punishmental-
ists. We join the Chippewa in understanding that the stars are
where we dance with our forebears in heaven. Carl Sagan on *Cosmos* even agrees with us.

In my place on the outskirts, where we do not enjoy market
share or megaphones, we queer religion quietly and consistently.

Here I want to address my Thumbtack readers. I will try to
tell them that "no mention of God" is a sneaky form of open-
minded censorship. Promising "richer, poorer, sickness, health"

vows imitates the unconditional love of God. Or higher power. Or ultimate reality. Or that which is larger than anything we are or will ever be.

Unconditional love is what marriage tries for—and fails to reach.

My son plays ultimate Frisbee. I think marriage is even more important than ultimate Frisbee. It involves the ultimate. It also needs a third partner, something that is even more important than your earthly partner. That partner is unconditional love and it can go by any name. The couple needs not promise to believe in God so much as to trust in unconditional love. That trust creates the perfect triangle—enough reach for the sacred as we make sacred promises and acknowledgment of what we don't know about who God is. We know simply and actively that God is in love with us and that we are in love with God—and each other. In that order. This proper placement of the humans in great life-giving intimacy is what marriage is all about. Why marry? To try to live a holy life and to unconditionally love at least one person, the way we want to be loved. That love creates good parenting as well as good sex as well as good lives. It is not penultimately important. It is ultimately important. God needs much more than to be mentioned.

QUESTIONS TO PONDER

1. How would you answer the question about God and marriage?
2. What if a guest at the ceremony is offended by God language?
3. If one family wants lots of one kind of God and another wants none, what might happen?
4. How does one demur about the divorce?

5

What's Sex Got to Do with Marriage?

IF YOU AREN'T MARRIED, YOU CAN'T BE AN ADULTERER. ONE OF the biggest promises we make when we marry—in the great majority of culturally agreed-upon terms—is fidelity. "Cleaving only unto you" is the fancy Old English way of saying it. Sex has a lot to do with marriage. Many men admit that they are nervous about marriage because they don't want to give up their "freedom." We know what they mean. Increasing numbers of women feel the same way. Often, marriage is the rite of passage where we stop fooling around and start committing. Commitment can be very scary in a world of pornography, a world of hooking up, a world of "me too," and so much more pressure to hypersexualize self and other early and often.

Sexual mores have really changed and then changed some more. We are almost "shoulded" to be sexually recreational whereas very few years ago we were "shoulded" to be very careful about having too much fun, too early, or outside of wedlock, or wherever. "Where Is Our Paradise of Guilt-Free Sex?" is the title of an article by Helen Lewis, in *Atlantic* magazine. She argues against pornography and its awful impact on women and men. I don't want to get into the major arguments on all sides of this important matter here. They do, however, matter to what happens to sex in marriage and therefore what happens to sex in a couple where the "rules" were different in their personal formation. Lewis argues, "Our language still lacks the words to describe the many varieties of bad sex that do not rise to the criminal standard of rape or assault."[1] What she means is that pornography can actually lead to bad sex, even inside a loving relationship or marriage. "Cruelty, shame and guilt are part of the human experience." Also, she says, "As long as our own desires remain mysterious too, sex will. It will not be good, not all the time. As long as some people have more money, options, and power than others do, sex will mirror the culture."[2] She fails to mention the threats to reproductive health that also end up in the marriage bed.

A marriage, traditional or posttraditional, that doesn't have clear agreements about monogamy and cleaving, recreational and procreational sex, is pretty much a fiction. Shared agreements about how to have sex, when to have sex, how to enjoy sex, how to "do" sex matter to people in a marriage. Clarity of promise makes everything smoother. When both people feel powerful about intimate interactions, the marriage is happier. Where marrying outside your tradition comes in has to do with the clarity that may be present in the religious and secular cultural traditions incarnate in the individual. Many secular people are mightily confused about fidelity. Likewise, religious people are mightily confused, with this caveat: they have their tradition behind them in promoting fidelity. But these traditions may differ widely. When you lose a clear tradition behind you (and, yes, secularity is a tradition with its own rules), you can get lost quickly. Having two with which to tango can be excruciating. She may think one thing, he another. Likewise, in a same-sex or transitioning or queer couple. Suffering, rather than joyful sex, can ensue.

The Christian tradition affirms the body, only to engage in mightily punishmentalist rules about sex in our side of marriage. I think of this passage:

*Therefore, I urge you, brothers, in view of God's mercy, to offer
your bodies as living sacrifices, holy and pleasing to God—this
is your spiritual act of worship.*[3]

The Bible says much more about the pleasures of our God and
so much less about fidelity that it is quite surprising the restraints
that people imagine on sexuality and the sharing of its pleasures.
The Bible is rarely understood well.

Some religious people, including me, have contracts with their
beloveds about monogamy, usually ones that omit the promise of
fidelity explicitly and intimately. We don't broadcast it but our
beloved knows.

I wrote a nonmonogamy appendix to our promises because I
was very confused about sexual fidelity indicating possession. This
was forty years ago when Warren and I married. I had also left
my first marriage, the one from my girlhood, because I fell in love
with another man. I knew it was wrong, and I didn't know how
to love the man I had loved and the one I fell in love with. Long
story. TMI. I wondered if I was just polygamous and that was that.
I needed to do my independence thing out loud. I didn't want to
promise something I knew I might not be able to do. To me, marriage was too holy for that dishonesty to infect it.

My premarital agreement about nonmonogamy was a religious
decision, not a secular one. I felt that I should only make promises
I knew how to keep. Promise was the religious direction; sexuality
came inside that. Oddly, my "prenup" gave me the freedom not to
be owned, not to make the same mistake twice and to enjoy fidelity.

Marriage has so much to do with sex and so much to do
with marriage that it is very important to clarify the promises.
You might even find out some funny things along the way on the
tremendously intimate path of getting to know each other. Who
wants what from the sexual part of the relationship? How simpa-
tico are what I want and what you want? What happens if we want
different things? Wouldn't it be nice to know sooner and not later?

When Luis Alberto Urrea spoke to Krista Tippett about his family, he said, "The Mexican-US border drove a divide right down the middle of my parents' marriage. My father had families [emphasis on the plural] everywhere."[4] We knew what he meant. Don't you also wonder what Luis's mother felt? For real?

Adultery is not always a broken promise, but it usually is an unstated-out-loud promise. Sex is about promises and clarity of promises.

Father Cedric wrote *Je vous pardonne tous vos pechés*, a collection of French priests' observations about the sacrament of confession.[5] Confession, they say, is often the most boring thing in the world. "When people don't like what you say, they leave and try their luck with the priest across the way."[6]

As a Protestant pastor, I also hear confessions but in a different way than the priest might. In the early years of my ministry, I often heard stories from older women who were almost waiting to find a woman pastor to say that they had been victims of incest as girls. Why would they confess that? Because they still felt like it had been their fault. And I've often heard admissions of incest, often from people at the end of their lives. The men (never a woman in my experience but I know that happens too) just wanted to relieve themselves of the burden of what they had done. As one of the priests says on this same subject, "I've always wanted to punch them [the incestualizing ones] in the face."

One of the stories in the priests' book absolutely amazed and amused me. I'll tell the story first and then tell you why.

"Once when I was a young priest, a couple came. She first. Cheating on her husband with a man, a friend of the couple. Then it was the man's turn and he admitted that he'd been cheating on his wife with a man also a friend of the couple. I realized as he spoke it was the same guy. The man was sleeping with his wife's lover. It wasn't easy to keep from bursting in laughter."

Why do both of us find this so funny? Because so much that goes on in a marriage is so fused that you can almost bet if one is cheating in one way, the other is also cheating in another way. She may be withholding sex or "blow jobs," he may be with-holding using a toy to help her with her orgasm. Or some such pattern. Cheating is not just adultery; it is on a spectrum of withholding. Both partners retreat from each other when there is not deep honesty in the promises. How to get the capacity for deep honesty? It comes, as I have been arguing, from a spiritual sensibility, a sense of salvation in the old-fashioned word, a sense of security, safety, trust, belonging, in the newer versions of that clunky word. Because God makes us so safe, so accepted, so for-given, so secure, we can tell someone else anything and he/she/they will still love us. Or try to. And if they can't, we still have a foundation that is larger than our partner's failure to uncondi-tionally care.

Marriage is a relationship with three partners, and the most important one is God or whatever is ultimate to you. We get all gummed up whenever it is just the two of us. We become idola-trously dependent. Sex becomes something that can't fully bear what we want it to bear. We need shared ultimates, shared values even if one of us is Christian and another Muslim.

If you find yourself attracted to someone else, isn't it sexy to tell your marriage partner? Isn't it interesting to talk about why that might be true? And to discover that (duh) everything is not always just right or perfect between the two of you? He is not perfect. You are not perfect. Your last husband wasn't either. Flirta-tions with others are a great subject for date night, if we are secure. It is a disaster if we are not. Change, people often say, proceeds at the rate of trust. So does intimacy.

The nature of a good partnership sexually, intimately, and in all the other terms is something like what Ruth says to Naomi so powerfully in Ruth 1:16: "Where you go I will go. . . . Your people will be my people and your God be my God."[7] These two women marry but not in the conventional way, only in an unconventional way. They promise to worship the same God, to have the same values. They promise to walk on the same road and to think of the same thing(s) as more important than even their remarkable love for each other.

They also marry each other's traditions or "people." Mature, generative people know how to marry. The trick is the honesty of the partnership, married to the third silent partner in the relationship. If God is too much for you to stomach or say, I understand. But the search for that which is larger than the relationship is fundamental to not overdoing or idolatrizing the relationship. No human relationship can bear the full freights of the promise of unconditional love. We will inevitably fail at it. We have to borrow energy to even try. We often say that marriage imitates God's unconditional love and is the closest thing we will ever get to it. We will also never fully get to it. We will fail at it. That is a given.

So many confuse religion with authoritarianism, nativism, prudery, general thuggishness. They think religion is about "believing in God." It is not. Religion is about trusting something that is larger than yourself to bless you and the promises you make. That's where the energy to keep promises comes from: in the dependence on the large and not the small. Religion by necessity needs to become more plural, as a way to respect the many faces of God. Pluralism about religion is the opposite of authoritarian belief or orthodox adherence. It can be a spiritually rich, particularly effective way to lift human dignity and run a coherent society. It can also be a great adventure in finding out what is really, actually, truly the most important to you. If its name is God, great. If its name is Force, great. Something, somehow needs to be more important than either you or your partner or your relationship. It needs a bucket in which to catch itself and find itself.

Marriage is a place to work and rest and to have fun. There we are "bound back" and moved forward. Remember, religion is a kind of bondage, a chosen bondage, a decision to belong to your partner. Our lineage may have become religious manyness.

Of *many*. That transition need not separate us from God. It could instead move us toward God. It can be a place where we are not just touched but moved. A good marriage has as its agenda each partner fully empowered to be their best selves and their most generous. It agrees on a purpose for marriage that is larger than fulfilling each other's "needs." It avoids that kind of economic, contractual, consumerist arrangement on behalf of a constant gift giving that imitates the divine economy. One is contractual; the other is covenantal. The covenant is a sacred promise, not a secular promise. We persevere at this constant gift giving because we want this kind of world so much. We desire it with every breath. Our maturity makes it possible. We also want to love something and someone unconditionally and to know we are loved that way too. We want to bask in that level and kind of security.

The biblical writer James presents perseverance as an artist, with our own souls as its medium: "Perseverance must finish its [the gospel's] work" in us, that we might become "mature and complete.8 Salvation, ultimate forms of security, form and shape a kind of wholeness in us that comes as a gift. It is the gift creation intended for us from the beginning. Have you ever felt like you missed your mark as a human? A good marriage can help you be a better archer. It can refine you and help you rededicate yourself over and over. A good marriage can complete you. Who doesn't want completion?

There can also be good divorces. In her book *The Good Divorce*, Constance Ahrons defines a good divorce as "when both partners and all children emerge as well as they were before the end of the marriage." I would love to conclude this part of this chapter saying that one-half of marriages are amicable.

THE DOLLY MAMA

I sometimes write as the Dolly Mama, a series of irreverent comments on important subjects. Here she goes off about sex. Enjoy.

And learn to think spiritually about sex as you prepare to marry inside or outside your tradition.

Dear Dolly,
Who said that there are only two items that get our full devotion and attention, sex and prayer? Is everything else a distraction? How to manage? How do we live a good life while so totally distracted? What should I do with my divided attention? Can I be genuinely intimate with another while so distracted?
Should I have more sex or worship more or both?

Divided

Dear Divided,
How do you worship now? A Sabbath walk? Friday night Shabbat? Meditation daily? Do you pray five times a day and get down on your knees on your rug? Prayer in the morning and before dozing off? Singing in a community? Sending a pledge to a community? Sunday morning services at ten or eleven? Weekday vespers? Advent or Lenten observances? Only Christmas and Easter or Yom Kippur and Rosh Hashanah and Passover? Drinking beer with friends at five? How would you evaluate your level of undivided attention to the Almighty? Do you think it needs a dusting? Or a makeover? Are you divided by time to pray and time you'd like to be praying? Is that the central distraction?
What is the noun "sex" to you now? Is it also a verb? What are your sexual habits? Do you think they need improvement? When/if you engage in sexual behavior, is it by yourself or with someone or someones, sequentially or otherwise? How undivided is your attention to your own pleasure or orgasm or touching?
How is your cat involved if you have a cat? In other words, are there erotic moments that excite you and cohere you

and undivide your attention that might not go under the label of sexual?

Have you ever read about the eroticization of everyday life, wherein you take enormous tactile pleasure in your surroundings? For example, the feel of sun on your skin. Or stars outside under a blanket with a pillow. Or weeding. Then the raking after the weeding. Or back to worship, when you do get an open afternoon, do you take a walk long enough to forget what time it is? What are the times when you are watch-free, clock-free, free free? Is that like worship or sex?

Have you ever heard the word "liminal"? Places of undivided attention are also called liminal. In sex we lose ourselves to another. The French call it the little death, la petit mort. *Liminal space is sometimes also described as the thin space, where we feel at one with the cosmos while remaining the specks that we are. Specks: very small matters in the larger scheme of things.*

Intimacy is different from sex or worship. It is the sharing of the liminal with another. In marriage, for good or ill, we hope to have a few liminal experiences. In worship, we hope to also have liminal experiences and connect with God.

In the liminal space, each participant is continually changed and made new in relation. Intersubjectivity is as good a name for the unconditional love of marriage as any other, even though it is a very clunky word and Dolly Parton herself would never use it.

As Martin Buber and Emmanuel Levinas have taught us, intersubjective space is holy. They mean it is a place where we are both subjects to each other, mutually, a place where we are not objects or objectified.

We bring all our conditionality and share it with another. We weave an honest narrative that names suffering, violation, and conflict for what they are even as this narrative articulates the grounds for our shared hope. When people marry, they have already likely told their tale of rape or incest or violation or being dumped or being put down by the guys subtly, regularly, on the job. They have likely told their story of some lover thinking they were fat or not "good in bed." They felt heard. They felt understood. It is not just women who have these stories to tell, by the way, but it is more often women in the relationship.

I recommend an action-reflection approach to all these matters surrounding attention and distraction. Again, Dolly Parton would never use that language I learned in school. She'd just say think first, do second. Act, then reflect on what happened. The reflection is the undivided space undivided. Then, after you genuinely orient yourself after the disorientation of distraction, you reorient yourself toward a cycle of paying attention to yourself. It sounds complicated, as though it were three motions, but it is really three parts as one motion. That kind of attention is already undivided. You just don't always know it. Prayer is reflecting on your action, in the presence of whatever you call God. It is a sigh. A breath. A give-it-a-break moment. It is being whole, not torn apart or torn into parts or macerated. First you, then the other, then God and then back again in one motion.

It also feels long, even though it might just be three hours or twenty minutes. It is when you are clock- and watch-free. If you are always acting, try matching the amount of time you are reflecting to the time you are acting. Everything will slow down. God will appear. Love will appear. Eroticism will appear, along with some true meaning for the word "orgasmic." You'll find yourself smiling, even laughing.

Dolly

Dear Dolly,
Is it true that boys are raised on pornography and its wide availability, and girls are raised to have something "kinky"

WHAT'S SEX GOT TO DO WITH MARRIAGE?

in their bag of tricks in the event of a make-out session after school?

I read a great article and it really got me thinking. It was titled "Is Sex Positive Falling Out of Favor?" by Michelle Goldberg, New York Times, September 25, 2021.

In the article, philosopher Amia Srinivasan describes teaching Oxford students about second-wave antiporn activism. She assumes her students—for whom porn is ubiquitous—will find an antiporn position prudish. They do not. They are more like Andrea Dworkin, who famously found sex-positive sexual behavior for women highly problematic, even as much as sex-negative counsel was.

The main reason the students cite for their distaste of porn, both the men and the women, is that the attention to emotion gets lost.

Her article concludes, "Old taboos have surely fallen, we need new ones. Not against sex, but against callousness and cruelty."

So, am I still sex positive or is that just a joke? What if I don't like pornography and its lack of emotion and its kinky, technology-sounding feel? Am I a prude? It sounds like I might have some company at Oxford, so now I can let my dirty little secrets out.

I do get "horny," as though I were a large mammal. I mean the language, not the feeling. And I am multiorgasmic till midnight with the proper partner, approach, music, perfume, sex toys, and the like. The more I trust my partner, the more able I am to find the deeper pleasures of which my various private parts are capable.

Also, what is a good number of times to have sex per week when you are twenty? Thirty? Forty? Fifty? Ninety? My mother swears there is one couple in her assisted living "home" that has sex every Wednesday afternoon at three, next door to

*her room. That's when hubby visits. My mother enjoys their
pleasure too, even though my father has been dead for years.*

*I have other questions about sex, actually, a lot of them but
I'll stick to just one more.*

*If my husband is having an affair and doesn't tell me
about it, is that worse than his not having the affair at all?
Which is worse, lying or cheating?*

Large Secretive Mammal

*Dear Large Secretive Mammal,
Is this a real problem or is it something about which you can
do nothing? What if sex positive means enjoying sex on your
own terms? It sounds to me like you don't even know your own
terms.*

*If emotional connection and honesty are important to you,
who says it is prudish not to require them, actively, sexually?
"Prude" is an old-fashioned word. Sexual positivity is as modern as fresh bread. It is also possible due to the widespread
distribution of birth control, if not abortions. Abortions will
return to the women's health care agenda. People just aren't
that stupid. For now, stick with birth control because it is the
foundation of the recreational sex you want to enjoy, inside an
honest marriage, with an honest partner, where both of you
feel good.*

*When my oldest son turned twelve after having three sex
ed courses already in his public school, he famously said to me,
"Mom, what's the deal? Can you just give it to me straight,
like in a sentence or two? I can't stand learning the names for
body parts anymore."*

*"OK," I said, taking a deep breath. I was a virgin parent
having the "talk" for the first time.*

*I said, knowing my son and his commonsensical brevity
if not terseness:*

"Rule one: Nobody gets hurt. Rule two: Consensual. Rule three: No babies."

He slept in a bunk bed then, on the bottom. I found these words in his terrible handwriting, scrawled next to his pillow, taped to the wall.

Rule One: Nobody gets hurt.
Rule Two: Consensual.
Rule Three: No babies.

He knew the meaning of the word "consensual" but hadn't figured out how it connected to sexual experience yet.

His son, my grandchild, said to me one night on a walk to get ice cream something very similar, many years later. He was eleven. "Bubbe, I am in love with a them. Mom said you would understand." Well, I did. He was so excited, he was literally jumping up and down. "Should I ask them out for a date or tell them I love them? What if they don't love me back? Wouldn't that be a problem?" He answered his own question. "I think I'll just love them quietly for now."

Next time I saw him, he had told them. He did not take his own advice but then again, who does? They told him they don't love him back. He said it hurt a minute but for now, he accepted their choice. "Dad said it had to be consensual." And, yes, they loved another friend, a mutual one. Ouch. This is called emotion connecting to sex.

Later that second visit, my eight-year-old granddaughter said, "Bubbe, I have to tell you something. You have to read this book [about lesbian girls]. I like girls. Not boys. I like girls. Mom said you would understand. Should I tell Papa?" I don't know why Papa got such a bad rap here, as he, like me, is sex positive about all kinds of different kinds of sex. And he married me, even with my prenup.

Anyway, I hope you see the need for approval in emotion-laden sexual activity, young and old, straight and not. Approval is a form of the unconditional love that eventually shows up in good marriages. Along with honesty and emotion, sex becomes postprude.

Dolly

What's sex got to do with marriage? A lot! That's what.

QUESTIONS TO PONDER

1. Can you and your partner write your own Dolly Mama question and answer it?
2. Is there anything so unmentionable between you that it needed humor?
3. How to write a Dolly Mama: Ask an obviously provocative question and answer it in the same way. Make believe you are a popular gossip columnist.

6

What's Romance Got to Do with Marriage?

Alain de Botton,[1] founder and educator at the famous "School of Life," wants to give romanticism a bad name. His videos and his teachings are more than convincing. He describes romanticism as a kind of innocence about life, something for teenagers, not adults. He will make you think. I can't recommend his videos highly enough. He joins Margaret Mead in imagining marriage as a more mature partnership. She advised that people not marry until they wanted to have children. Before that, she argued, we should live together. And if we don't want children, why marry at all? The famous anthropologist predicted the two-tier marriage that we have now, where young adults live together for a long time before marrying. That is the new normal, whereas my mother would never have approved. And here I want to disagree with both of them, respectfully.

Children are not the only reason to marry. That makes marriage a bit of a tying of the knot of obligation around our necks. It turns children into a form of obligation as well when instead the best parents are fond of their children and enjoy them. Some are even amused by their children. Likewise, romance is possible for adults, not just "children."

What does romance have to do with marriage, particularly marriages that may be adding a thick layer of quick mutual discovery about diversity, a problem no culture has fully solved yet, much less intimately?

Marriages often start in romance. Don't you love to tell the story of how you met? How you were turned on to something about him or her in a singular way. Perhaps it was the way he looked into your eyes, poured you a second glass of wine, pulled your chair out, touched your hand—or the way she listened to you, asked questions about what was important to you, reminded you of some wonderful memory? Or when you found the *one* on the dating application and squealed with others about it before you even met the person? Surely, there was something funny in your "myth of origin" as a couple.

The more often we can tell this "first date" story, the better. (I'm going to attend to all the changes in dating soon, just not right now.) That story will bind us. Marriage is belonging to one another. It is the shared memory, possibly differently perceived, but nonetheless the time we *met* and how marked we were by the meeting.

After romance comes the dishes and the diapers. The recriminations. The regrets. The disappointments. One wag says that leadership is disappointing people at a rate they can tolerate. So is marriage. It is not just folk or funny that people talk about marriage as a noose around your neck, that both parties have a "bachelor" party where they drink a lot and premourn their freedom.

Which is better: resist romanticism from day one or gradually combine the romantic and the pedantic? What about an answer that says both? Date night is a marvelous intermediate place to live. An evening a week for romanticism? Why not? Romantic experience does not need to be a steady diet. It is often quite wonderful to be married to your best friend. Still ... many of us have been tutored to be special, very special to someone. It's fun.

When was the last time you got dressed up, went out on a date, and came home to make love? That's romance. When was the last time you got mad about something the previous evening and made a good joke about it the next morning at so-called breakfast?

Romance is great, but it is not going to last. You can hope for some romance in your partnership but likely hope for something larger as well. Having a common goal—like encouraging the other to be their best self vocationally and spiritually—will deepen the romance and wash the dishes without developing (too much) enmity. Having a common goal of shared power, so that each feels fully sovereign in the relationship, can go a long way to keep things exciting and sexy and romantic as well. Knowing what you imagine the meaning of life to be *together* can also be a lot of fun. You are so much less alone in your pursuit of your beauty, your bliss, your purpose, your destination. Even if the most significant other is only along for the ride, at least they understand what it is that you are "about."

As soon as the inevitable power differences arrive, a repositioning needs to happen. Likely, that will not happen just once but sequentially, over and over again. How? When the lines of communication are wide open, things remain exciting. Margaret Mead also said that she was married to the same man three times. She knew that her partner had changed, would change, did change.

Examples include one being very happy with their job or workplace or work associates at exactly the same time the other may not be. That can shift over time and even reverse. One can have a much longer commute; another can abruptly get fired. One can raise children with ease; the other can have an anger management problem or just plain need a lot more sleep. Being able to talk as friends as well as lovers will make a mountain of difference in keeping each powerful and agentive, while each welcomes change, activates change, anticipates change, and, most fundamentally, talks about change.

Therapists call this talking "bidding." When our intimate partner, lover, friend, business associate bids, they may say something like this: "You don't seem like yourself this week." "I notice a diminished interest in seeing that friend or that show or that movie or going to that meeting or church. Am I right?" The sexiest thing in the world is to be noticed, seen, recognized, observed, not objectively or judgmentally but subjectively, tenderly, carefully. Your partner may know things about you that even you don't. Then again, they could be dead wrong. A marriage where bids remain unbidden is likely to dry up on its vine. A good marriage is where bids are practiced often, regularly, with full chance for the observed person to question the observation. "Nope, you are seeing something very different about me. Let me tell you what happened or what really happened."

Sometimes the worst thing that can happen in a marriage is that the sex gets forgotten one too many times or someone neglects to notice that someone else got a haircut. My husband was going through a very rough patch and managed to forget my sixtieth birthday. Normally we throw big dos for each other on our zero-ending birthdays. He just forgot and I was too angry to tell him he was in the active process of forgetting. He ended up throwing me a whopper of a party for my sixty-first, and we had a great time at it. (His amnesia about my birthday had nothing to do with his being Jewish and me being a Christian pastor.)

Still and nevertheless, practicing bids intimately can help people from two different traditions manage their diversities. How do you want to raise the children? Do you want to worship or go hiking on Sundays? How will we have any weekend or any holidays if we both attend Advent, Hannukah, and Christmas, or Eid? How can we balance the power so that everybody gets some of the participation they want, some of their heritage of values recognized? What do we do when one is so down and the other so mad that they don't even negotiate the delayed birthday party? Why didn't I just mention it early enough to hear what he was feeling about "one more thing"? Why? Because I wanted to punish him. Maturity is almost never a full-time habit. Yes, I am an antiperfectionist, not a perfectionist.

Bids also evaluate, and they do so organically and regularly. It may not be that romantic to question whether our December holidays or April holidays or spring vacation "worked" to achieve its intended relaxation or deepening. But absent that kind of regular evaluation of experience in a normalized way we won't get to know each other, we won't manage diversity well enough to really get to know the other. Really being "known" for who we are is the bliss of marriage. It is romantic plus, not just romantic. It is romantic plus intimacy, romantic plus unconditionality, romantic plus generativity, romantic plus love, and romantic plus trust. Romantic can coexist with dishes and diapers. It is a both/and.

Obviously, there are stages in a marriage, just as there are stages in life. I call the senior stages of life "early, middle, and late dotage." If you have a better word, use it. I think there are similar losses along the way earlier as well. There is early marriage, middle marriage, and late marriage, if you are lucky enough to last. In early marriage, the process of discovery prevails. It is very romantic to seek and find the other. In middle marriage, things can easily get dull. Multiplying bids and asking a lot of easy questions can keep things interesting. Long marriage has its own splendors unless people have gone in different directions, sleep in different beds, keep different schedules, enjoy different things. And are into punishing each other for previous rejections. Long marriage is having someone around you who remembers a lot of the good times (and bad ones) that you do.

Date night is a funny device. It is often on Friday night. It often starts to fit like an old shoe. That restaurant, that movie theater, that walk, that parking space. Sometimes, couples shake up date night by adding a time with their friends, either at a ball game or a spa. Sometimes, absence does make the heart grow fonder. If the time famine is keeping us from having other intimate relationships, and we only "date" one person, that can likely create some conflict also. The nuclear family and the marriage relationship are not meant to carry the full freight of life or friendship. Having other strong relationships—perhaps as couples but more likely as individuals in some form of women's group or men's group or basketball game or tennis game or golf or cards or mahjong— is almost as important as date night. These additional pleasures take the pressure off date night to be perfect. Pick your pleasure. Encourage each other to pick their pleasure. Take turns picking. Simultaneously, "push" your partner to have lots of fun, not just a little fun, and most certainly not just with you.

Many people feel tension around their families of origin. These tensions may interfere with date night scheduling if you let them. It is very important to train your extended and nuclear families about you and date night and when it *will* be. The sandwich generation is not a joke. The Christian family may have one set of expectations, the Catholic Italian family another, the Jewish family a third, and the secular family a fourth. Whatever combination of diversity your family has become, getting to know its expectations for visits, for holidays, for spending money, for lending money, for taking care of each other's lawns or properties, no matter the size of the expectation or obligation, you need to know it. Most preferably, you may want to interrogate it. You may want to establish boundaries. We'd love to come every other weekend. We would not love to come every weekend. These matters of time and money and energy are not matters of romance; they are matters of negotiation. They may be especially difficult for people with different origins. Romanticize negotiation? Yes, why not? Is not the point that everybody gets the most of what they want? Making that kind of authentic destination the goal of negotiations is very loving. It can feel more than warm. We can go to genuine gratitude that we have such a good friend as well as good romantic partner and lover. When expectations for timing and seeing each other are super clear, it is very easy to break out of the pattern in the event of an emergency or special birthday or occasion. Once the pattern is established, it will be easy to maintain it as well as to interrupt it.

When matters of how to relate to the outside world of family, or work, or pleasure are not discussed in loving, careful environments, they easily become the fodder for fights. Your mother again? Your brother-in-law again? Creating the freedom to fight about how you spend your time, energy, and money—using the power of persuasion, the power of compromise, the power of alternating what you do and how you do it—these are very real matters involved in marriage. They can be fun in a trusting relationship, and they can be horrible in a nontrusting relationship. In a trusting relationship, both partners are profoundly encouraged to pursue deep thinking, to change their minds, to have a moral imagination about what is going on. These patterns of trust building are the way individuals promote their inner and outer life in community and intimately. Building these patterns of trust is not necessarily romantic. Instead, it is the prelude to the romantic experiences you do want to continue to have.

When there is no romance, we move into a stage of dangerous incoherence, where we can't agree on anything. We have no carrot. We feel invisible. We lose our way. When one loses their way in a couple, the couple also loses its way. Negotiation may not be romantic, but it is the romantic's best friend.

BACK TO THE DATING GAME

The purpose of marriage is to protect and anchor the individual so that he/she/they can become their optimal self. By optimal self we mean fully self-actualized, fully generative, fully mature. We mean agency, self-direction, personal authority, being ourselves. We mean self-regulation. We mean personal power to be our best selves. We mean equipped to be our best selves and to achieve the values we adore. We mean great clarity about what we want and how we are going to get it and what resources we need to achieve these objectives. One resource we need is power. When we date, we look for a partner who also wants power and for whom we want power as well. When we date, we look for a partner in these optimal patterns for the self and therefore the union.

In a perfect world, both partners would enter the dating game with sophisticated and mature understanding of what kind of marriage they want. They would be clear about their destinations. Unfortunately, the term "blind date" is more likely to occur. How could we possibly expect young adults and/or late teens to know what they wanted the rest of their life and to only date toward that objective? We go into the dating game at a young age for the most part. We do marry our mother or our father. We often marry in young, immature ways because we marry when we are young and immature. These systems are not going to change anytime soon. We can improve them by knowing a few things in advance—and still end up on a blind date, thinking that we are sighted.

In saying that marriage yields the optimal selves of both partners, I am not setting up a ridiculous objective—like being careful not to fall in love while you are still young. By optimal self, I do not mean perfection. I mean optimal. Many of us pack a suitcase full of woundedness into our wedding bed. It comes packed in the same baggage as our immaturity. We will never be perfect. We will always fall back into our lesser self. We are humans, not Gods. Why do I spend so much time talking about sharing power and each person feeling that they have plenty of power? Because having power to become our optimal self is the clear path to becoming that self. Power arrangements change over time, just as we do. The more power we can achieve early in our lives, the better we will be prepared for the latter parts of our lives.

If our marriage partnership robs us of power for these destinations, we will neither become our optimal self nor assist our best friend and lover in becoming the same. The goal is to maximize each other's power to become their best self. Thinking these kinds of thoughts before we open the dating app is a great idea, which is unlikely to happen.

There is a new partner in the dating game, and that is the Internet. No one knows yet if it is going to promote or discourage interfaith marriages or marriages outside of the tradition or even promote power-sharing marriages that end up with mature, generative human beings as their result. What we do know is that it tries to ask questions about power, meaning, vocation, and spirituality and often asks more questions about money, status, education, race, and class.

If you surf the Internet, you can find hundreds of dating sites. They all select in a certain way. RightStuffDating.com helps Ivy League college graduates find each other. They say they are "dating smart." There is a site called BookLovers.dating that helps you find someone who loves books. Over forty? Over sixty? Best sites for Christians? Should Jews use Bumble? Can Catholics find other Catholics easily on sites that are not supported by Catholics? Chinese dating? These are not easy questions if you are trying to find a partner. You engage in a process of preselection even before you press the first button on whatever site you use. I tried to shop for a site that would help me find a Christian mate, and all I found was some antiabortion material that then came unbidden to me for weeks.

An interesting way to look at the question of dating sites is to ask the questions that CNN asked: Should black people be allowed on all sites? Should they have to disclose their race? These kinds of assumptions about "like liking like" have enormous resonance. Since they are not the questions of this book, which actually commends and respects diversity in marriages—interfaith, interracial, inter, inter, inter—I will leave my opinions about dating sites behind. I am not just not an expert on them; I never used one. Thus, my humble critique as an outsider.

For now, if you are dating or on dating sites or divorced and newly looking for a partner, ask yourself these questions: How important is it to you that you marry inside your religious tradition? Or racial tradition? Or age group? Or an American if you are one? Or an Italian if you are one?

If you were married for five years and had a two-year-old child who suddenly died, would you want to be able to pray with your partner? How important is prayer to you? Very few marriages survive any injury to a child. Someone said to me yesterday as he talked about the suicide of his thirty-year-old son, "I'd like to laugh again." Five words. There is an entire life wrapped up in those words. If he and the mother of this child get along, share power, know how to bid, have some romance in the bank, maybe their marriage can survive. If none of these factors were on the dating site, we won't be surprised. They aren't. And I would love to be wrong.

This chapter is about what romance has to do with marriage. You can't necessarily guarantee a marriage that stays romantically alive for decades or one where great sex prevails every time you feel like it. You are more likely to have a marriage that begins in romance and ends in something like respect or comfort or best-friendness. The singer Bono said it best: my wife of forty years is my best friend and she is my best date. How lucky can you get? If you are lucky or play hard at it, you could be lucky enough to have all of these in different doses at different times in different years. Notice I said "play" at it. If you are working at it, you are probably already in a lot of trouble.

When you answer the question honestly about what you want if you are still dating and looking, be very careful. You may prefer a Christian now and a doubter later. Or vice versa. You may enjoy the profile of an ex-monk who says he wears a T-shirt that says, "Whiskey and yoga." You might not want to marry either whiskey or an ex-monk.

More and more people don't really know who we are religiously in the first place. Sociologists differ between old-style American "external pluralism" involving multiple religions within the society and "internal pluralism" involving multiple religions within individuals. We experience the effect of both in culture, marriages, and ourselves. While we are nowhere near a melting pot, just as globalization has not yet wiped out all ethnicity, still the trend is toward blending in the populations we know. This blending underlies the seismic liturgical shifts we are experiencing. Not only do people move between time zones, sometimes daily, in their work, they also move in what the Dutch architect Rem Koolhaas calls a zone or moving fluid space. Blend joins motion to create a new kind of people; we can't be surprised that such a new people would birth a postsanctuary, post-Sunday, or post-Saturday liturgy. God may even like blend better than homogeneity. There is no reason for dating sites to have a fluid catchall phrase for the name of our spirituality—but then again, maybe that would be a start.

I might call myself a blend of Christian Orthodox, pagan, and postdenominational. My children all identify as Jewish. My husband is Jewish. My parents had no doubt they were Lutherans. I know I am not alone in spiritual confusion. That is why I would never ask a dating site to manage me or my confusion. Instead, I might want to know in my mind and heart, both simultaneously, that I want a partner who wants to walk a spiritual path with me as well as a financial one, pray with me as well as praying to vocation or what kind of house we eventually buy. I remain very interested in the house, the vocation, the date nights. I don't see them as opposed to my spiritual orientation. Instead, I see them as part of it. That is my point here: Such clarity is not only romantic. It is romantic plus and it can be achieved even after blind or digital dates resulted in a marriage. It can even be fun.

Practical Approaches

1. Study dating sites like you are buying a car. Shop around. Price them out. Notice what they feature.
2. Don't let yourself go. The old-timers know what that means. It means the man who puts on a lot of weight and doesn't care,

the woman who forgets to wash her hair. It means not caring about what you look like because you don't think your best
friend cares. Why not care?

3. Don't confuse romanticism with gorgeousness in cultural terms.
   Confuse romanticism with tenderness, attentiveness—and give
   it as much as you want to receive it.

4. If you date digitally, become smart about what information the
   site wants from you. Don't just disconnect because someone is
   not from your race, tradition, or class. Use dating as a diversity
   exercise: get better at it.

5. If you date digitally, be careful. There is a lot of date rape out
   there. You don't want to get hurt.

7

What about the In-Laws?

WHEN WE MARRY, WE MARRY AN INDIVIDUAL AND A FAMILY that used to be the fundamental family for the person we marry. They lose someone to us. No matter how much they like us, we remain a kind of culprit. We are the agent of change. We therefore marry the family as well as marry the individual—and we marry them with their loss being the first thing they experience of us.

It is not accident that so many jokes feature the subject of mothers-in-law. We are terrible. Those of us who birthed sons are very likely to be terrible. The likelihood that the woman our son marries is going to like us also is relatively small. Oedipus does rule, internally in the mother, the son, and the wife.

I've always wondered why fathers-in-law didn't get the same treatment or be as frequently the fodder for jokes.

Blended families are the new norm. They "happen" to people who marry within their traditions and outside their traditions. By blended we mean families that might be of different racial or religious backgrounds. We also mean stepfamilies and those who have more than one family. What is excruciatingly interesting about our subject of beyond tradition is here. When problems happen in a blended family, the first explanation is often racial or cultural. "If he just had married someone like us. . . ." By "like us" you can mean never divorced or always one tradition. The blame explanation is convenient. It may or may not be true, but convenience is the champion value of our day. It is always more convenient to have an enemy than to have a friend. It is rarely easy for people to befriend trouble or diversity. It is much easier to blame diversity for trouble.

As one Jewish mother said to her son, "I didn't survive Auschwitz for you to marry a shiksa." Ouch. After you get done understanding her bluntness, you still want to wonder what in the world is going to happen next in this family. There may be a separation of the married couple or a separation of the son from his family. That kind of separation is a likely outcome, unless something big happens, like growing up or learning how to live beyond your tradition.

Biological invasives come to mind. They are real. They are everywhere. No one likes them. We also don't like insects. But both invasives and bugs are part of the evolutionary pattern, just like postcultural marriages are.

When one of my favorite nine-year-olds was baptized in the backyard of his house, it felt just right to me. Let's call him J. Loving. Blended family was all around, reminding him that he belonged to them. He was just putting away his water-shooting pistol so we could get on with the ceremonies. It was a Super Soaker. People asked each other if someone had remembered to bring the bourbon for later. It was a casual afternoon with a serious purpose.

The Catholic grandmother and Protestant grandfather were divorced. Both brought their new partners, one of whom identified herself as a proper pagan and the other said "nothing" as the spiritual denomination.

The baptism was so different from my own, even though the meaning was the same. Mine was exactly seven days after my birth because Missouri Synod Lutherans believed if you died before being baptized, you might risk going to hell. I was wearing a baptismal gown that had arrived from the Bohemian section of Germany, near what was then Bohemia, close to Italy. All the country borders were different, so no one really knew. The white faded baptismal gown had been worn by many others. It arrived in the US at Ellis Island.

I gave it to my baby brother, now deceased, for him to use to baptize his son, my nephew. My nephew can't find it. Maybe out near where the Super Soaker is? Not only has blend taken over families, dilution has taken over religion.

When our twins were baptized in our backyard in Chicago, and we didn't know anybody, and the twins were a surprise, we named them children of God, children of the Jewish faith, children of the Christian faith. We assured them that they belonged to a religion and to a tradition that didn't exist yet. The Unitarian minister who lived across the street did the water deed. We didn't have a church yet. We used tap water. They squirmed. We were more remembering the meaning of the matter of their unexpected birth than realizing the meaning of the matter of baptism or religion or belonging or blend. (Yes, you can get pregnant while nursing a six-month-old.)

Words matter. In all these baptism services, we agree to be chosen by God. We agree to belong to God. We agree that the community standing there, whether in shorts or not, is our own. We get written in the Book, as William Faulkner's character Dilsey says. Our name is in the Book. All these ancient meanings show up at the party, invited or not, understood or not.

During COVID-19, many of us had better dreams. We remembered a kind of depth that had dissipated. One columnist said, as the virus got weaker for a while, that "the city is Rip Van Winkling into wobbly wakefulness."[1] When we have a little time to think, we go to the heart of matters like baptism or belonging to a family or having in-laws. We do an ancient ritual "differently." In a backyard at age nine, or in another backyard blending Jew and Christian in ways that you make up as you go along. Yes, these ways dilute both of the ancient faiths. They are also seeds of the new.

The words in naming ceremonies are important. Often these days, we carry the names of some people who went before us. We are "named" after someone. These some ones may devolve into mother-in-law jokes, but they don't begin there. They begin in wanting to be connected to the past. Rituals link us to the past, no matter their content or their depth.

In the beginning of our lives was the word. At the end will be the word. The word is belonging.

As noted above, baptism is essentially a Super Soaker. It soaks you with your old tradition or your new tradition or your future, during which time you might be alone. It is the word of God made water. The word of God can also be some other symbol. It doesn't have to be water.

We say in a baptism or a bris or a naming ceremony that when all else fails, remember your baptism. We named you as belonging. If we you were Dan Brown in the *Da Vinci Code*, we would say, remember the Grail. If you were Ta-Nehisi Coates in *The Water Dancer*, we would say remember the conductivity. The family's genes literally carry the family's traditional homes and words to the next generation. The energy flows from generation to generation, and blend doesn't stop it.

We hope children will remember the choices made for you in your backyard or church or synagogue. You made the choice to believe to accept God's acceptance of you. To belong to God who made a choice to belong to you. These matters don't need the cultural specificity of a tradition's words so much as they need the words and the ritual. These can be clumsy or sophisticated or classical or each in different ways. The point is the stopping to pause to ritualize the child.

Another picture of an extended family follows. This one is a family that is all Baptist and underwent a serious change. I write about them often because they are exemplary of a post-denominational experience. Basically, the very wealthy patriarch of the family fell in love with his secretary. I know it is a cliché.

He then got cancer three years after leaving his wife and four teenage children. The first wife decided to befriend the second wife "for the sake of her children." Wife two took the day shift. Wife one spent the same several months taking the night shift. Why tell such a story? Because they learned how to be different, to move outside the accepted norms of their traditions, to move into a new way of being, "for the sake of the children." When one of the children from the first marriage died, it was the two wives of the same man who took care of each other, quite beautifully. They had become friends. They were also postcultural, even if all Baptist.

People imagine that there is only one way to be married or to baptize or bury, what we call in my trade "hatching, matching, and dispatching." That is not true. There are many ways to ritualize life's transitions in blended and nonblended families. When we marry outside our tradition, we get to chart our own path, find our own way. The way is less clear. Still, and nonetheless, we marry a family and a tradition as well as an individual.

Likewise, there are problems that are particularly related to people in the queer community. One family of origin may be accepting of a queer way of being, the other may not. Usually what happens is that all the in-law problems disappear in families that are not accepting. They go underground. Whenever a family "disowns" someone, they remain a nonpresent but silent partner in most everything. When we marry into a family where some-one has been exiled or thrown out, the family still lives on in the excluded individual. Another kind of in-law problem replaces the usual one of the interfering, "too close" one.

Repeating: when we marry, we marry a family, not just an individual. We may be marrying a tradition not our own but no matter what we marry into a tradition. If we do have children, those children carry both traditions along their ways with them.

There are very interesting problems that are very particular to postsecular marriages or marriages where one person is secular and the other is not. The mother-in-law matter wears a different costume but comes with the same oedipal psychology.

The place where these psychologies and their different costumes are most likely to end up is when one of the parents of one of the members of the couple dies. Does your tradition always take the widow or widower in and his family always go to assisted living centers? Knowing that before you marry may be the best thing you can do for each other. And by the way, there is no always in a family's pattern, especially today. More likely whatever happened in the last generation has turned into an always, despite there being fifteen previous generations, each of whom might have done something different regarding their elders.

One of the most interesting trends today is that of accessory apartments, small spaces that act as full living sites for the elderly in the family, that both keep the elder close and allow distance for the nuclear family. They are also used as places where people can have live-in help in terms of childcare or cleaning services or secretarial help. Accessory apartments allow for a kind of architectural decision for the retired elderly members of the family. They make compromise possible and also make for fewer "mother-in-law" problems.

Often, the burden on the nuclear family from a new generation, likely an elder, creates much pressure for the married couple. The biological son can feel terribly guilty if he is not taking care of his mother or father, while the nonbiological daughter-in-law can feel quite jealous of that care. The scenarios multiply, all different, all unique, all something for which we cannot prepare enough. While dating is the best time to discuss such matters, very few people do. We are much more likely to talk about whether we both want to have children than what to do with our aging parents if one dies. If? One will die before the other. That is for sure. Your choice will be much better if it has been made prior to the crisis of death. And elders will be mightily blessed to be involved with such decision-making before they need help or shelter.

Finally, it is very important to understand that not all elders or in-laws are problems to married couples. They can be blessings too. Elders have a lot to add to families, if allowed and invited and trained so to do. We can also be a pain in the neck. As with everything else, the more maturity, the more generativity, the more talking honestly and out loud, the better. If families can develop honest conversation about hard matters, they can thrive. If they cannot, they will not thrive.

Julian Is a Mermaid by Jessica Love is a delightful children's book that might help with all these intergenerational matters. Abuela (grandmother in Spanish) is the hero of the story. Julian, a boy, decides to become a mermaid. The illustrations are stunning. They flow from one color to another as though that kind of flow was normal. While Abuela is taking a bath one day, Julian dresses up like a mermaid. He turns himself into a girl. Abuela is astonished. She gets herself together. She gives Julian some pearls and takes him to a parade of mermaids. She walks Julian into the parade. As we all know, Abuela could have behaved differently. She accepted the future for and with him. She didn't have to be accepting of gender fluidity. She could have chosen the past of her tradition's values instead of its future. When families go into the future together, it can make all the difference between thriving and not.

QUESTIONS TO PONDER

1. What is your favorite mother-in-law joke?
2. How were you baptized? Was your partner baptized? Did it have meaning? Did it take? Does he, she, or they belong to God?
3. What will (or did) your parents think about your wedding? Did they feel at home? Do you know what their wedding was like?
4. What pattern do you want for your relationship with your in-laws? How will you get it?

8

What Kind of Sin Is Divorce?

MARRIAGE BINDS US TOGETHER. IT IS A SPIRITUAL BINDING, A spiritual attachment, a coming together of two families, two bodies, and two spirits or souls. Its purpose or destination is the mutual enrichment of both people. By mutual, we mean a constant sharing and increase of personal power and agency in both people.

We come together to become more ourselves. We come together sure that our lover will also be lovely, that he or she will bring out our best features, our best work, our most witty self. We come together assured that the other will always want us to have more power and to be more in charge, even and especially in the relationship itself. We marry to generate and to be generative. We marry to mature. We come together with great anticipation and enthusiasm; we separate with a thud.

Everything gets very quiet; no one competes to tell another story and laugh once more before the evening ends. When divorce happens, we unbind. We untether. We unknot. We pull apart. We become like a ball of yarn that no one cared about for a long time and that takes a long time to ravel, after unraveling. We become distant, which is the opposite of close. Divorce removes us from the path of maturity and generativity and confronts us with a kind of stagnation. We missed our mark. We weren't our best self. We know it takes two to tango. We became distant from our God or our Dao or our path. We fell apart. We no longer had a place.

As someone who has been divorced (in the passive way of putting it), I remember the hours and days and years of misery. Once in love, we came apart at the seams. We tore each other and we tore ourselves. (Jews have a service called K'riah, in which we tear a piece of fabric ourselves to imitate the death of a beloved.) We went from a nice pattern of days and a nice story for our lives to not knowing who we were or what to do next. All the furniture moved, and it wasn't just couches or chairs. All the rooms were rearranged and almost all the doors were locked tight. The windows wouldn't open. The holidays refused decoration. They became assaults on the heart. I remembered what kind of tree he liked and the way I faked liking tall, skinny ones too.

My dear friend Pat, who had never been divorced, finally helped me out, after the therapists and lawyers definitely did not. She said, "You'll wake up one morning and realize you're not thinking about it and that's when you'll know you can move on." She was right.

The suffering of divorce is often the failure of two people to find a way to stay together. Very often, divorce is the right thing to do, if the two people are hurting each other more than one or both can bear. The language I used above about being off our path, not being our optimal self, being distant from our God or the Dao or our path is language for sin. Lots of people want a definition of sin.

Here are the best ones I know, combined into a ball of trouble. Sin is missing the mark of your true humanity. Sin is being distant from your God or Dao or path. Sin is being on the path that is not your path. And sin is finally a kind of falling apart, a lost way, being lost. When we sing the song "Amazing Grace," we know both lost and found, sin and saved. "I once was lost, but now I'm found. Was blind but now I see."

Some suffering is essential in the human life. I've never met anyone who hasn't suffered. Some suffering is also unnecessary. By optimizing our spiritual capacities—our freedom from sin—we can do things we didn't think we could do, like love more than we thought we could, or forgive more than is just.

The direction I provide here to the unnecessary suffering has to do with having more agency, not less. If you are already divorced once, this chapter won't help you much. But if you are thinking about divorce, perhaps it will. You might suffer less if you can find more agency, more power, more personal purpose, the kind that just might release the same spirit in your partner. No guarantees, please, as there are none.

The chances for unnecessary suffering increase when people marry outside their tradition. People who marry outside their tradition divorce more than others do. One out of two marriages today ends in divorce. The figure is so high because most people marry more than once, upping the odds of a fissure. There is widespread agreement, supported by data, that when like marries like, marriages stay in their married state a little longer. Like means the same political party, the leading indicator of stable marriages; similar economic backgrounds; same or similar race; and then religion. My goal is to equip the reader to be a change agent and not be overwhelmed by the mixed-upness of intimate life, with families of origin, current partners, and children's religious and spiritual preparation. Think mother-in-law jokes and how to move beyond them.

Of *course*, marriage is a site of conflict. It is a site of conflict because it is a site of love. Anger is a form of love. As stated in the Introduction, you can't have love without conflict—and intermarriage creates even more conflict for marriages than marriages within the tradition do. This book loves all love and especially loves the love that exists amid diversity of origins. Its purpose is to enjoy and affirm marriage outside your frame of reference, while helping those marriages reduce the possibility of unnecessary suffering.

If a friend or relative of yours has been divorced, which also means that they were spiritually stranded or possibly were into the hole of addiction or indifference or both, you will have heard these themes in their talk with you. They will know what they did or neglected to do. They will rarely feel blame-free. They won't know how to smile for a while, much less how to be happy. They will partially blame themselves when they are not blaming their former partner. They will talk of missing the mark of their true humanity. "I wish I could have been more forgiving" or some such. They will speak of getting lost, being off their path, not knowing what to do next, not having their needs met. They may speak of being abandoned by their higher power, whatever that is. They will wonder if they will mature or how they will go on, alone.

Is divorce a sin? The answer is yes. Sometimes it is a sin. Sometimes it is being sinned against. Usually, it is both in a taut and tight tangle. The way the word "forgiveness" is used in the Lord's Prayer is what most marriage counselors already know. Forgive us our sins as we forgive the sins against us. Forgive us our debts as we forgive our debtors. Forgive us our trespasses as we forgive the trespasses of others. . . . This is what we mean by it takes two people to ruin a marriage. The answer to keeping marriages happy (not longer, but happier longer) is in more spiritual agency, not less.

When you marry outside your tradition, you might have a good long talk about difference as a way of at least getting your percentage against a "failed" marriage a little higher. People don't marry to get divorced. No marriage is truly a failure. For its time, it was likely life giving. It was certainly a learning experience. Often necessary suffering matures us. Unnecessary suffering is another matter. Often, unnecessary suffering strands us spiritually into an ongoing chaos. Just remember this while you are dating: One out of two marriages today ends in divorce. Interfaith and interracial marriages have a higher percentage of divorce. Marriage is always a risk and when you marry outside "likes" you increase that risk. Diversity involves risk—and also carries the blessings of risk. When we marry outside our tradition, we risk being blessed by our courage. And we reap the rewards of understanding.

DIVERSITY TRAINING

More and more employers require diversity training. Clearly, we all need it. In it we learn how to avoid microaggressions and how to enjoy microaffirmations or microkindnesses. Couples would do very well to take one of these courses, just to learn how not to have a pointless fight about whether there should be both a menorah and a Christmas tree in their apartment building's lobby or town square. If you differ about this matter, it is great to know that before the wedding. If you don't differ a little about matters such as this, you are likely in a state of denial about diversity.

Couples might also read *Attached: The New Science of Adult Attachment and How It Can Help You Find—and Keep—Love.* Attachment theory is the well-established thesis of psychology dating back to the mid-twentieth century dealing in children's bonds with caregivers. It remains in Amazon's Top 200 books today. Why? Because it shows the types of attachments for which we all have propensities, based in our early childhood experiences with our caregivers. There are three categories: about half of us tend to have secure attachments, about a quarter of us have anxious or ambivalent attachments, and another quarter have avoidant attachments. Up to 5 percent are disorganized, vacillating between styles of attachment. These matters are as important as political affiliation, economic background, racial identity, and religious identity. They are also cultural in a way. When two people who both avoid attachment marry, they may want to know that before they buy a house that has a mortgage or have a child together.

Like in Myers-Briggs tests, Enneagram typing, and zodiac signs, these kinds of variations of personal orientation really matter. Couples who want to decrease unnecessary suffering do very well to pay attention to inherent diversities and to learn to enjoy and affirm them rather than fuss, consciously or unconsciously, over them.

Some people don't really want a long-term relationship to start with. *Attached* advocates marrying someone with your attachment style, so that an avoidant does marry an avoidant.

Suffering comes from a fundamental immaturity around concepts like these. They matter as much as religious orientation does. Unfortunately, religious orientation only "orients" us. More and more people have moved beyond or outside of their religion of origin. More and more of us are postdenominational or postsecular or disappointed with our version of Christianity or Judaism. We start a little stranded about religion. We know what it means to have a political party, although we may be disenchanted with that as well. Race is biological as well as cultural. Economic origin and its blessings or its origin can't really be changed. Once a person has been poor or rich, they don't forget what that means to how they look at money. Religion stays in flux—and that flux can be a strong asset when it comes to marrying outside your tradition. Religion is both a past while enabling you to choose a future.

Religion is that constellation of things that establish, maintain, and celebrate a meaningful world. It includes practices, rituals, Christmas trees, menorahs, never eating pork, and many, many more habits. At its best, religion is fundamental trust, not really belief, which is different. Belief implies the head's assent to concepts. Trust comes from your belly. Trust allows you to suffer without losing hope. Trust allows you to forgive what is unforgivable. Trust borrows the power of the divine when the self's resources are insufficient. "Religiousness is a leaky business which refuses to be quarantined," quips a famous scholar. "It won't be pinned down or boxed in."

Marriage is about belonging, binding, coming together, becoming more connected to our values because we have support and rituals to support a best friend. It borrows God's unconditional love, which says nothing can separate us from that love that grounds us but that we do not own. Sickness and or health, rich or poor, better, worse. Religious and spiritual people know we do

not have the capacity to love unconditionally. We try and we fail. Those destinations, if not realities of trust, get us to spiritual maturity, generativity maturity, the best life has to offer. Many even feel incomplete without a partner, someone on whom to practice staying on a trusting path.

"I wrote my own vows, and to be on the safe side, I wrote Evan's too," says a famous *New Yorker* cartoon. Our failures to keep our promises of unconditional love can be rooted in good old sexism, or the overfunctioning of one partner and the underfunctioning of another, or plain old sin. Even the best marriages fail at something. Even the most fully mature generative power-sharing individual fails at unconditional love, every now and then. Marriages that start on a spiritual level have a better shot at the universal trust in the universe that makes mistakes possible, predictable, and opportunities for renewal, not falling apart. What is a spiritual level? It is the place where God's created diversity is appreciated, not just tolerated; it is where we love it so much that we can't imagine living without it. We work at learning about diversity out of love for the "other."

SOMEONE HAS AN AFFAIR

Consider the most likely reason to divorce. Someone has an affair. Another lover triangles his or her way into the heart of a partner. Or someone falls in love with their work instead of their family. It's never the affair; it's always the cover-up. The litmus test for a good marriage is whether you hide your conflicts from your partner. The hiding will break up the marriage because it doesn't trust the partner to understand. Trusting your partner to understand will create trusting interactions, which will prevent affairs. Not always, but enough of the time.

I was fascinated by a workshop at the American Religious Association called "Architectures of Hiding: Crafting Concealment." It's about what a building hides as well as what it shows. In a good marriage, very little is hidden.

Architectural creation, its representation, interpretation, and associated activities more often than not are seen as processes of revelation. However, one can argue that architecture hides as much as it reveals. "The Purloined Letter," a detective story written by Edgar Allan Poe, describes the chase to look for a stolen letter with confidential information. The story revolves around the search for a letter hidden by being left out in the open. Poe highlights a complicated relationship between visibility, revelation, clarity, and its complementary hiding, concealing, camouflaging.

Trust in something larger than yourself allows you to trust a partner. You wouldn't want to stay concealed forever. Sometimes you use tricks as good as Poe's purloined letter to stay hidden. But is that what people want out of life? Don't we prefer to be seen?

SUFFERING

Because the majority of Americans live what can only be called a sheltered life, compared to the rest of the world's population, we suffer differently. The most acute suffering most of us will experience will be in the world of our intimate relationships. There we will fight, quarrel, cry, punch, and struggle along on a pathway that too often results in bitterness. We may even feel shame about our failure to sustain an intimacy. Shame joins blame to be a fairly common feeling among otherwise well-cushioned people.

If you have already started to feel blame in what I say, perhaps that proves the point. I grew up poor, became middle class, and at this rewiring, retiring moment in my seventy-five years of life I feel very guilty about how much security I have. I don't understand why others don't. I know it was not because of anything I did or because I worked hard or harder than others. I know my relative wealth has nothing to do with my own efforts. Lots of people work as hard as I do, have similar gifts and talents, but not everyone got as lucky as I did.

Blame and shame are lame. For years I blamed my mother for not leaving my abusive father. She took his punches. She had

also been nearly drowned by her mother, my grandmother, when she was three. My grandmother was institutionalized in a mental hospital in the 1920s. Now, due to the grace of God, I quip that there is a lot of mental illness in my family and then I grin. "I have no idea how I can be so healthy." Yes, I am fully joking and trusting God and my partners in conversation to get the joke. Anyway, my mother clearly had some attachment issues. She was raised by my grandfather and an aunt. Still, I blamed her and left home early just to get away from what I called her passivity. After my father died, and after she had finally left him to go on and enjoy the last thirty years of her life living happily with my sister, I said to her, "Mom, why didn't you just leave him?" She replied very quickly, "Because you three kids would have been brought up in a shelter. I stayed for you." I trust her honesty. I trust mine. I don't have to agree with it. But I knew that Elly, her real name, which is not Mom, was supported by her God through all of it and she did what was the right thing for her. It's none of her business or even mine that I disagree.

"I just want you to shut up, God says, and let you know how much I love you," thus says my guru here, Brené Brown, on the unimportance and overdoneness of shame and blame and the way they cause unnecessary suffering.

Buddhists often argue that "while the far enemy of connection is disconnection, the near enemy is control." I was trying to control my own mother's morality. Why? Because I was not grown up enough, then, to know what I know now. Human beings can make choices. We can choose connection, or we can choose control. Control gets in the way of connection. Connection yields much more control, agency, power, and security. Why go small when we can go big?

HOW TO GET HELP
Your pastor is probably the last person you're going to tell about your drug addiction or your extramarital affair or the fact that

you are miserable around your partner most of the time. Why? Formal spiritual advisors are widely ridiculed as judgmental fools. Holier than thou is our middle name. These stereotypes may not always be true, but they are often enough to keep people from telling us their secrets. Thus, when it comes to spiritual care we need to be careful of the experts and trust the amateurs. More so, we need to become self-care experts. By all means, try to find a spiritual care person—a rabbi, priest, minister, therapist, coach, or all five! But let them teach you how to care for yourself. When we learn to care for ourselves, we will learn to take care of others. And we will be less afraid of the suffering of others and more open to it, as well as our own. The golden rule really matters: love your neighbor as you love yourself. Your neighbor is yourself. You are your neighbor. Your partner is your closest neighbor. When marriage therapists tell you to treat your partner like your highest-paying client, we mean it. We don't mean satisfying their contracts on time. We mean caring for their spirit. I have often joked that every not-for-profit organization needs a chaplain who spends all their time caring for the spirit leader of the organization, even if that is the custodian. Think of your partner as your spirit leader. Be their spirit leader. Trade gifts often. And I don't mean just flowers or date night. I mean attending their spirits. Care for them.

Care is different than fixing. It is mightily different than fixing. Care is engagement with the story as it is, not the story as you want it. Joy is also wanting what you have not, wanting what you don't have and likely can't get. Spiritual care is something you do because you want to do it and you may do it, not because you must do it. Care that you must do is contractual care. Spiritual care is covenantal care. You choose its love and its participation in suffering. Children are always going to break our heart, even if they do nothing but move out of the house and go to college. Why? Because we love them and we never want to let them go—even though love always involves letting the beloved go.

At least three commonsense rules apply to spiritual care.

Don't use the word "should" on yourself or the beloved. "May" is a good substitute. "You may quit hurting yourself," not "You should quit hurting yourself."

Don't try to fix people. You are not a repairman. You are also in need of repair. Relationship is better than repair.

Just say, "Tell me more." And listen. Really listen. Don't spend your time thinking about what you will say or do next. Just "tell me more."

My beloved husband always adds a fourth, borrowed from Alain de Botton, one of our gurus: "Sometimes you just have to be deaf."

There is no perfect English counterpart for *mudita*, but the closest we can get to its definition is the idea of "sympathetic joy, unselfish joy, taking joy in the success of others," and to Buddhists, this is "pure joy, unadulterated by self-interest." This is not a temporary, transient, cheerful state. This is a deep practice of embodying joy through solidarity with the joyful thriving of one another. And in this country's current climate, *mudita*, unselfish joy, is a form of blessed, messy resistance. It burrows deeper than the surface happiness our capitalistic crust tells us we should pursue. Christians think of *mudita* as the peace that passes understanding, the success of unconditional love that refuses control. *Mudita* starts and stops in refusing to try to control things and starting to try to enjoy them as they are.

I want you to remember a saying from a beloved Hindu guru, Nisargadatta Maharaj. Again, I needed to go to another faith tradition to get a fresh take on our own tradition. Isn't it wonderful that Christianity doesn't have to be our only resource, trapped in some self-satisfied, whitewashed vacuum? This guru said: "When I look inside and see that I am nothing, that is wisdom. When I look outside and see that I am everything, that is love. And between these two, my life flows."

Date Night with God?

If you want a marriage that survives divorce and resists a boring pattern, become spiritual caretakers of your soul and each other's soul in a delightful tether. Yes, you will need a community of practice, a set of rituals.

If you want to be a caretaker of your own soul and that of your beloved, my first piece of advice would be to keep doing what you're doing, which is to "shop around." Find a community of practice for the couple that you are. Try everything; then find something that joins date night in being a time of spiritual reminder of who God is to you and for you. Think of it as shopping for a beautiful, comfortable couch, not just something that you might need. Shop as though you are really desperate for the right-priced, most beautiful couch. Maybe it is nothing more than a book club or a tennis league, but it needs to be communal, honest, and a place where you are at spiritual home.

It might well be that you are more comfortable in a small community that is less hierarchical, like a bowling league or a house church or a group of monastic associates. But those kinds of communities aren't easy to find—sometimes you have to know somebody to find a small community like that. Instead of trying to join a church or find a community of practice, see if you can find a centering prayer group. Instead of joining a Buddhist sangha, look for a group of people who just like to get together to meditate. It might well be that a practice circle is all the community you need. I believe contemplatives need community, but you don't need institutional religion to find a meaningful spiritual community. Likewise, not all institutions of religion are failures—and many are realizing that they have failed and are trying desperately to reform themselves (ourselves). They/we are looking for you as hard as you are looking for us!

I was surprised at my strong reaction to an advertisement for Olay that was four pages in the *New York Times*. The first full page said, "Do Something. We Can't Open Your Jar." The second page said, "We Heard You." The third and fourth page were a rollout of a new jar that is easier to open. I think of the religious institutions I tend exactly this way. We need to do something *different* that helps people open us to our best selves.

While you are looking, try to cultivate friendships with like-minded persons online. There are so many Facebook groups, for example, that are organized around a shared interest or belief. If you like Richard Rohr, join a group devoted to his teachings. Krista Tippett's "On Being" is my favorite. Or a group devoted to centering prayer, or Celtic spirituality. Once you find a group that feels like home, see if any members live in your vicinity. Meet someplace neutral or safe (a coffee shop, perhaps) and see if there's potential for friendships to develop. Maybe your spiritual community will be something brand new that you help to create. Marriage outside of your original tradition will only be improved by creating new traditions, new ways of supporting people through intimate life and all of its joy and sorrow.

Finally—going back to the marriage analogy—if the day comes that you find a community that you truly feel at home with, take the time to try to be as honest and realistic about the community's shadow side. Can you live with it? If you can, then prayerfully consider joining that community. Recognize that, sooner or later, the community will drive you nuts—just like even a healthy marriage will at times drive both spouses to distraction. That will be part of your spiritual practice: learning to live with, to manage, to make peace with the limitations of the community. Because every community has its limitations.

Meditation is so popular at NYU in the chaplain center that it might be good to rename it the Center for Meditation. It is surely not a center for spiritual life—because spiritual life includes ritual, community, democracy, music, sacred texts, really great choirs and really terrible choirs, really great and beautiful self-governance, and a lot of trivial e-mails flying through the cloud. I happen to love meditation and am more often meditating than not. But meditation is hyperindividualistic. You go so deep inside that you forget there is an outside. That is the point, right? It is highly effective at keeping a person calm. So is just about any attention to the inner life. But deep calm of the inner person is often on behalf of something outside. Like work. Or singing. Or communing.

I know why people have turned to meditation and away from the communal aspects of religion. I have seen congregational meetings where people trivialize the presence of God or spirit or the importance in their actions. I am old enough to know that these very difficulties almost always are the death that brings life, the trouble that brings triumph, the trivial that turns important.

The only way things ever really improve is when humility rears its powerful head in the conversation. That's one of the great things about Jesus. He appreciated the loss the old were experiencing while also changing things. Yes, he got himself riled up every now and then in the dry and dusty temples of his time. But mostly he advised and embodied a loving humility that asked the temple of his time to change. He did not survive Auschwitz himself. He also brought one shiksa after another home. And finally, he didn't brag about how great he was—but advised people to go low to get high, to be servants to kings, to lose to gain, to get small to get large. He also advised full union of the inner calm and the outer courage. The individual inner life mattered to him and the outer communal life mattered to him. That's why Christianity is such a great religion when it is small and such an awful religion when it goes imperial.

Casper ter Kuile and Vanessa Zoltan cohost an interesting podcast program called *Harry Potter and the Sacred Text*. On their website it is stated: "This podcast creates time in your week to think about life's big questions. Because reading fiction doesn't help us escape the world, it helps us live in it. Each week, we explore a central theme through which to explore the characters and context, always grounding ourselves in the text. We'll engage in traditional forms of sacred reading to unearth the hidden gifts within even the most mundane sentences. On this podcast, we ask: What if we read the books we love as if they were sacred texts?"[1]

Sacred texts help us navigate the complex and chaotic world around us. Similar to the bleeding of sacred and secular borders in our postsecular culture, they have gone outside and along with the traditional sacred texts we most commonly think about in our Abrahamic traditions, as well as others. In the postsecular young adult literature genre, for example, one may catch a glimpse of the distinctive religious and secular in its "authoritarian" and "emancipatory" aspects. Contrary to common expectations of our postsecular times, many contemporary writers who guide the struggles of our young people still seek the "hidden life," participate in "the symposium of the whole and engage with agencies of desire, meaning, truth, and yes, Spirit with the troublesome, rebarbative capital letter."[2]

I find this most interesting in the study of some young adult literature where there is a "struggle between self-fashioning on the one hand, and historical determination on the other, and it is the tension between the autonomy of the individual and the shaping pressure of history that the political ideology of each novel lies." This same tension in a child's spiritual development and religious struggles, often characterized as misfits, creates a separate religious reality outside the attempt to maintain order. Christian Smith, in his work *Soul Searching: The Religious and Spiritual Lives of American Teenagers*, says that this is surprisingly in line with the majority of American teenagers. Smith argues that their ideas of religion, faith practice, and theological doctrine are completely outside the orthodox religion, even though they may profess one of those religions.[3]

It is no accident that divorce rates have increased along with religious deconversion or disaffiliation. These are both phenomena that begin in the family, and are intergenerational in nature, with a history much longer than the coinage of the term "nones" in the early 1990s.[4]

The poet Rilke became famous by begging us to love the questions. Here I worm my way inside what Rilke means. He is not surprised that people have to be admonished to love questions. If it were easy, we wouldn't need admonishing.

I get uptight if I don't know my partner's plans for the evening. Or whether the budget is going to pass the congregational meeting. I don't love questions. I hate questions. One way to love questions is to give more permission to uncertainty. You might even become open and affirming about them and welcome the questions. Don't worry: I won't overspend my vulnerability budget. I will be frugal.

Also, could I date questions instead of marrying them? Could I welcome questions on my way to loving them? I do know how to be glad at the arrival of conflict. Whenever conflict, large or small, comes along, we are about to learn something. We learn nothing when seas are calm except how to float. When seas are churning, we pay attention. Communities of spiritual practice really help us churn.

Things seem so hard right now, politically, environmentally, and more. We search for trustable leaders under every rock. Disturbance drives us deep, below the rocks, into our cores. We are learning how racist our country has been. We are unlearning exceptionalism. We are learning how damaged we are by generations of permission to sexual violence. These pictures of a different country drive us to a hidden underground grail that flows near the center of things. We can welcome disturbance as something pregnant with good. We can worm our way to truthful acceptance of questions. We can learn to be our own trusted pastors. We can at least care for the soul of our best friend.

To attain intimacy, learn to trust. Learning to trust whatever God is to you is advanced by belonging to a good spiritual community. You won't marry God but at least you won't be divorced from the divine either.

QUESTIONS TO PONDER

1. What do you think about the word "sin," as defined here?
2. How have religious institutions helped you? How have they hurt you? Does anybody know the story you know about you and religion? Would you like to tell it?
3. What do you really think about people who have been divorced? Is the stigma gone in you toward them?
4. Review the book *The Good Divorce*, mentioned earlier. "A good divorce is when all parties leave the arrangement in as good an emotional shape as they were before the divorce." Do you agree?

9

Spiritual Preparation for
a New Way of Life

You and your partner may have a lot in common at the spirit level, the values level, the eschatological level.

Eschatology is the destination question: Where do you want to end up? Where do you think creation will end up? What is the destination of humanity and how do you fit into it? My hunch is that we will all be brown.

If you are lucky enough to stay together for your entire lives, one of you will predecease the other. You will know each other at the end the way you know each other from the beginning of your adult lives. Your endings will be your individual eschatology. They might also begin to end your tradition.

You may know each other better than anyone else knows either of you. And still, you will be pioneers. You will be biological pioneers if you procreate and have children. You will be cultural pioneers because members of your tradition even one generation ago may not understand you or your children or your brand of faith.

You will be firsts, perhaps reluctantly, perhaps intentionally. This book is about how you prepare to be firsts as a couple.

Many same-tradition couples straddle the gap between the faith that they grew up with and the faith they married into. Think of this down and dirty guide as a "catechism of the twenty-first century." It is especially for the structural diversity in your relationship but is also useful to the many differences that religion's metamorphosis is causing all of us, single, straight, gay, married, transitioning, and more.

Maybe catechism is too old fashioned a word. Let's try the Dolly Mama's Guide to Spirituality, an introductory course to what it means to be spiritual and religious, especially for people navigating diversity. By the way, if you are not navigating diversity, you might. The Dolly Mama is allergic to should.

The Dolly Mama is part Dolly Parton—irreverent, always light, with a giggle in her talk and a wiggle in her walk. She is also part Dalai Lama, a Tibetan monk who laughs a lot and leads revolutions in his spare time. In real life, the Dolly Mama is an ordained United Church of Christ and American Baptist minister. She looks a lot like me.

The Dolly Mama believes spirituality is not taught but caught. She is post just about everything but especially postdenominational. She has almost no patience with stale religion or stale bread.

"I'll tell you why I love her," said a Wisconsin housewife about Dolly. "Dolly is everything I ever dared to be. She's outrageous looking. But just once, didn't you ever want to do something outlandish? Without worrying about what everyone will say?"

In my unreal life, I get asked questions about fists and knees and American flags, sometimes all in one day. I like to say, "I just don't know." Then I like to say, "Do you?"

It's enough to frighten a person who gets paid to be preacher to her high-heeled boots.

GENERATIONS

When Jesus is born at Christmas, as the book of Matthew points out right at the top, people begin by legitimating him through his genealogy. Its point, likely, is to say that we know Christians had a lot of continuous, undisrupted history as Jews, for a long time. We come from somewhere—and into this history, this long history, something new has come. A baby, born of humans, representing God.

A 2017 Gallup poll finds that the percentage of US adults who belong to a religious institution has plunged by 20 percentage points over the last two decades, hitting a low 50 percent last year. This book treats marriage religiously. It respects the legacy and most of the lineage of religion. Not all of it but most. It does more good than harm. It also does harm, as many people would be glad to tell you. It also treats the breakaway people with spiritual respect. At least they are honest. They don't just follow the rules. It treats marriage as a kind of small *s* sacrament, a holy covenant made between two people in front of God; however, God is named or not named by them. In marriage we make promises before whatever is most ultimate and least penultimate to us. It is also sacramental in the way it is a cultural ceremony and ritual, witnessed by those closest to us. Dual religious belonging, for individuals and for couples, is more common than ever and soon will be the norm. I am already a renegade religionist with routes in lots of places, both pagan and institutional religion. I feel very normal.

Your wedding day may be the best, if not most expensive, day of your life.

It's a little like the many of us who go to Genealogy.com or any of the other sites that show your trajectory as a human—and going there and finding a sharp shift in the curve at a certain point. You were a Persian for thousands of years and now you are an African. Yup. That's some of what the gospel is trying to tell us. Not so much Persian to African or African to Ukrainian but something that big. We were people who had one kind of God whom we worshipped and loved and now we are to become people who have another kind of God whom we will worship and love. History has been interrupted—in a good way. From now on you will be different.

When history takes a sharp curve—when history is no longer continuous but instead pronouncing itself different—it is really hard on old people. We had Warren's college roommate in for the weekend—and he, like Warren, is Jewish. They put up our Christmas tree—which was a first for Marc, a practicing Jew. He was appropriately sardonic about it. And yes, one of the main issues in Christianity is the way it is supercessionist, which is a big word for thinking it is better than the Jewish tradition of its parent faith. That conceit is what I am talking about with regard to Matthew's first chapter. For a long time, we had all these folk. Now we have a new one. Ours is better.

Anyway, Marc told Warren a story, which I overheard. I have already mentioned this as a one-liner, like I've already let you get a glimpse of Dolly. Here comes the context.

One of his Jewish friends brought home an Asian woman to introduce to his parents. He was obviously setting up for an engagement. The mother responded to the son as follows: "I didn't survive Auschwitz for you to bring a shiksa into my house." In case you don't know what Auschwitz was, it was a place where Matthew's version of history—now we are better—went to a violent extreme, just like most lies finally do. In case you don't know what a shiksa is, a shiksa is a gentile, an outsider, not good enough for a Jew.

I think Jesus is really good, but I don't think he is better. I think he is instead different. Maybe that would be a way to enter the generations conversation once again. When younger people say they are different, it would be marvelous for older people to say "cool. Tell me more." When younger people say they are different, it would be great if they didn't necessarily act like they were an improvement on history. I am still ashamed for having chanted at age twenty-nine, "Nothing like us ever was." There are other parts of my youthful exuberance for which I am proud. That slogan is not one of them.

People for generations have needed religious institutions to help them get on a path toward goodness and stay on that path. Yes, we are led to the good by the imperfect.

You may be interested in spiritual preparation but frankly you'd like to work with someone who knew something about it. A good kidney doctor if you have kidney disease. Not an amateur. When it comes to spiritual preparation, we are all amateurs and always have been amateurs.

The perfect religious community does not exist. Finding a church is like finding a spouse. There are two dimensions, and both are equally important: "Can I truly love this person, and will they love me?" But just as important: "Can I live with their imperfections (and can they live with mine)?"

Every human being will sooner or later let us down. Every spouse will be, in some way, a less-than-perfect life partner. So, part of the spiritual work of a good and healthy marriage is learning to love each other despite both of your imperfections.

And often, a person's imperfections might be somewhat related to their positive qualities. The beautiful person who turns out to be narcissistic. The bon vivant who just can't manage to be faithful. The artist who can't figure out how to hold down a steady job. I know these are stereotypes! But I think there's a principle here.

When it comes to faith communities, the religious organization that celebrates intellectual freedom might turn out to be a very cold and emotionally distant group of people. The one that has a great youth program might not know how to educate its adults. The one with a strong emphasis on social justice might feel more like a nonprofit organization than a sacred place where the mysteries are adored.

So ... how do we find the community and partners we can love? And the one whose imperfections we can live with? By becoming fans of the funny, the obtuse, the difficult, the daring, and the new, that's how. Our ancient texts tell us that everything is always becoming new. Why don't we get over our false notion of safety hiding in our pasts and realize it is living in our future? We are in a continual present where we have small and significant chances to improve regularly. There are a few rules.

Rule number one: Shelve the word "should." If you can't shelve it, budget no more than five shoulds per day. Count them.

Rule number two for Dolly Mama's tradition: Surrender the need to be right about anything and everything at the same time.

Rule number three: Honor your lineage and your ancestors; give them thanks and respect. Then embrace the future. That's what they would have wanted you to do.

Rule number four: Creatively misadjust while also adjusting. Yes, you do have an adjustment problem if you live in the twenty-first century. You can't be serene in a world that is crazy.

Rule number five: Don't expect to enjoy being different all the time. Learn to love its questions.

I get uptight if I don't know my partner's plans for the evening. Or whether the budget is going to pass the congregational meeting. I don't love questions. I hate questions. One way to love questions is to give more permission to uncertainty. You might even become open and affirming about them and welcome the questions. Don't worry I won't overspend my vulnerability budget. I will be frugal.

Also, could I date questions instead of marrying them? Could I welcome questions on my way to loving them? I do know how to be glad at the arrival of conflict. Whenever conflict, large or small, comes along, we are about to learn something. We learn nothing when seas are calm except how to float. When seas are churning, we pay attention.

Things seem so hard right now, politically, environmentally, and more. As I write, the virus appears to be quite in charge of adapting very well to its hosts. We search for trustable leaders under every rock. Disturbance drives us deep, below the rocks, into our cores. We are learning how racist our country has been. We are unlearning exceptionalism. We are learning how damaged we are by generations of permission to sexual violence. These pictures of a different country drive us to a hidden underground grail that flows near the center of things. We can welcome disturbance as something pregnant with good.

Rule number six: This one is important because it sounds so unreligious and unspiritual. Learn to enjoy questions in community, not in homogeneous groups or even just family groups but in public. As my kids used to say, "In pub."

We can learn to enjoy meetings. My Pilgrim denomination, the United Church of Christ, is all-American in its love of democracy. That doesn't mean we are good at it. It just means that we love its potential. The UCC is said to be judged by the quality of its encounters. Isn't that a fancy way of saying a meeting? What might make us not give up meeting together? I said in the previous chapter that you as a couple will need a community that will also drive you crazy. Here are some ways to show up that resemble the way you might show up in your partnership:

1. Show up at the meeting with high hopes and be the most positive person present. You've heard people say that you should seize the interview? That's how you get the job. That's also how you come to enjoy meetings.

2. When negative people show up at the meeting with the full intention of making everybody else feel as rotten as they do, call them out. I mean call them in. How else can we spur each other on? "Misery loves company; miserable people love the company of miserable people."

3. Give every group three chances and then quit. But when you quit, realize that meetings are inevitable in the for-profit and not-for-profit worlds. David Whyte: "If you really want to kill yourself, nonprofits are the places to go." Why did he become a poet in residence at corporations? Because one executive realized that "the language we have in the for-profit world is not large enough for the world we have already entered."

If you don't learn how to self-govern in self-governing meetings, what will happen to self-governance and democracy? If you don't learn how to self-govern in a marriage and encourage the other to do the same, what will happen to the marriage? The stakes are high, not low.

Don't expect to be good at this kind of community building that is democratic and self-governing at its base. I arrived at my friend's house, where I was to stay the night, and couldn't make the keypad work. BLIX was the new access code except that there were no letters on the keypad, only numbers. I must have had some level of Alzheimer's because I thought about doing it in my head:

You know 1 is for B

5 is for L

Et cetera. But in the dark and the cold, I wasn't up to it.

I was in my hometown, Kingston, New York. I got a room at the Super 8 right across the train track from the better place. I intended to go into the main part of town to eat except that the sidewalks weren't completely plowed. Then I walked around to a place where I could cross the street, but the crossing lights weren't working. I shivered for about ten minutes and realized that crossing a six-lane street was not in the cards. Plus, I was right across from the busy bus station and kept thinking about my grandmother's death by bus at that station long ago, coming back from a bingo game, downriver. One bus after another was pulling out.

It was twelve degrees. Making a way when there is no way? All I wanted was dinner and soon to bed. I had heard lots of people encourage larger making of wayless ways and always nodded in a social justice–fed approval. But tonight was different. My paths were closing rapidly.

Then I decided to go back to the better motel, thinking it might have a restaurant. The Super 8 had cold coffee. When I got to the train track, a man came running up to me with a Santa hat on and yelled, "Stop!"

That's when the party train, the Catskills Mountain Polar Express, came through. Four cars. Lots of jollity and singing.

Apparently, it is a train that goes up and back to Woodstock and you can rent it for your party. After the train passed, I went to the better motel. I walked in like I owned the place.

There the entire chamber of commerce was having its holiday party and the restaurant was closed. I joined the chamber, got a name tag, and blended right in. The feast was spaghetti and meatballs and a lot of Chianti. Plus, the obligatory plates of Dusseldorf's Christmas cookies.

I met some of the people I was supposed to meet with the next day. They said, "I didn't know you belonged to the chamber." I said, "I don't."

The next morning, I went out to walk around, and the parking lot there was fully covered in black ice. Leak in the hose on the side of the building. A man came out with a dog. He was yelling at the dog. The dog was not happy. The man didn't see the ice and fell down and did not somehow hurt himself. The dog got off the leash.

I chased the dog, got the dog, and got someone to help the gentleman up who was still down, cursing the ice, himself, and the dog.

I think I saw him at the party the previous night.

Rule number seven: Fake it till you make it. Don't miss the trains you could have caught. Join the party, wherever you are. Or better yet, find the party. Worse, make the party. And get to the heavenly feast, even if it is only supper. Nobody's done this before. Why should you be good at it right away? Act like the future is welcoming you.

Before you say nothing can be done about your spiritual illiteracy or poverty, just look at all the other things we do regularly about which nothing can be done. There is a self-respect involved in self-defense. What the Dolly is recommending here is that you stop thinking of God as impossible, belief as impossible, goodness as impossible, fun as impossible, religion as impossible, and your in-laws as impossible. Make your spiritual starting point something right in front of you, not something way beyond you. Let God sneak up on you through an imperfect community, an imperfect partner, an imperfect you. An unexpected holiday party brought in by train. Honor your ancestors by doing what they had to do.

A good friend of mine's husband died, right after they bought a new boat, retired to a beautiful community, and were ready to play. He was only fifty-five. He suffered before he died. One of the ways she premourned him was to talk a lot about how she was going to have to sell the boat. When he died, she opened a letter from him. In it were ten prepaid boating lessons, with someone who would teach her how to steer the boat. I wish my ancestors had written such a letter to me.

One did even though we are not related. Her name is Rosie and she had painted a mural of the entire town on a kitchen wall in the parsonage. She was two pastors ago. That means two pastors had lived in the kitchen with the mural, which was fading away and starting to peel. Finally, we found a note from Rosie, written in paint on the inside of one of the cabinets. "Feel free to do whatever you want with this mural. I wouldn't want your art in my kitchen either." We took it down but only after several members of the community objected strenuously to our interest in removal of the folk art that dominated what was to be our kitchen. Wiser voices prevailed, and we were able to memorialize the entire mural in beautiful photographs that were enlarged and reproduced to be in the church and in the local historical society. Message: keep looking for the better people, the ones who are willing to get out of your way so you can find your way. They are there hiding in the kitchen cabinet.

There is nothing namby-pamby or sentimental or innocent about becoming a strong spiritual self, one strong enough to be safe and good simultaneously. Some call this spiritual resilience. I call it spiritual maturity. It comes from regular, usually silly spiritual preparation, day by day, week by week. We bounce back from the last injury in time for the next one. We also have fun along the way. Dolly calls it the low-cost form of personal entertainment that spirituality actually is.

QUESTIONS TO PONDER

1. Describe your overall education: kindergarten through your exit degree. Where would you place your spiritual education? Are you advanced or a beginner?
2. What would your partner say?
3. What do you need to know?

10

Religion Hasn't Changed, but You Can Change the Way You Are Religious

PERHAPS WE CAN HOPE FOR THE HOLY IN OUR MARRIAGE AS AN act of choice, instead of compulsion. I know it is individualistic to choose. Those of you who spent too much time in the enlightenment will be smart enough to figure out that I am offering an individualistic solution to the problem of the collective. Or the relationship. Nope. There is one more sentence on my topic above, "Religion hasn't changed, but you can change who you are religiously if you find the right companions." In other words, do it socially. Make a nod toward the holy socially, not individually. You can make the marriage you want. It is up to you. It is not up to your psychology or your education. It is up to how much Spirit you can find. And this is where marriage comes in. If you are a spiritual sleuth, or a seeker of Spirit, you can go on a hunt from a fellow traveler. The two of you together can make Spirit the fundament of your life together. Common values will take you a long way toward fun, promise keeping, love, and all the good things that most of us really want from marriage. The culture and the economy don't care if we achieve these values. They do care about making money off our attempts. The material is very powerful. It is also very neutral. It is a thing. We are spirits. We are breath. We are created.

You can't marry well outside your tradition if you can't marry well. They are the same cloth. The demographic changes that have us meeting and dating folk outside our tradition just underscore the difficulties and possibilities in marriage itself. If marriage is a sacrament, which it is, a sacramental act, something that makes holy the ordinary, then adding a difficulty to it, like diversity of backgrounds, is just the icing on a beautiful wedding cake.

Yes, different religious backgrounds think different things are differently important. That is obvious. But all major religions imagine idolatry, the putting of self before the ultimate. All major religions advocate promise keeping, as a pattern for unconditional love. All major religions imagine that nothing can separate us from our creator. Only us and our self-centeredness, which is actually off-centeredness.

For marriage to succeed and for "interfaith" marriages to succeed, adults may option to be mature spiritually as well as psychologically. Cultural proficiency is a form of maturity. Cultural delight in difference is a form of generativity, what most psychologists think of as the end stage of maturation.

But first clarifying your own personal relationship to your own notion of God or good matters. If you don't know what that is, you will be in a state of perpetual confusion. You don't need to buy the whole religious package or institution or even history, much less doctrine. You can lean toward the holy, which is ineffable in the first place.

Before we get to cultural proficiency, we need spiritual proficiency. In sum, spiritual proficiency is knowing that God is first and you are magnificently second. God loves you, the universe loves you, the cosmos loves you and therefore you may love it back. Imitating that love will give you the power to love another. Why not have that person be your life partner? Or your children? It is quite a relief to realize that you and your overdone self-consciousness are not the only matter in the universe. We finally relax. We feel that peace that passes understanding.

Erik Erikson, a powerful social psychologist on whom I did my master's thesis, put these ideas as follows. There are stages in the emotional development of the human. They are:

1. Trust vs. Mistrust
2. Autonomy vs. Shame and Doubt
3. Initiative vs. Guilt
4. Industry vs. Inferiority
5. Identity vs. Role Confusion
6. Intimacy vs. Isolation
7. Generativity vs. Stagnation
8. Ego Integrity vs. Despair

Generativity is an objective of mature life to him. Not just maturity, the capacity to control yourself, to take care of yourself, to defend and be yourself, but to give yourself away to something larger than yourself. That includes the love of your life in marriage and also your vocation and your children. Marriage exists to mature you. Marriage exists to create gratitude in you. Marriage exists for your joy. It is also a container for your failures. You are not going to succeed at marriage. You are going to get better at loving someone, as he, she, or they get better at loving you. Cultural proficiency is a part of this maturity. We stagnate when we don't love diversity.

Yes, my good friend's mother said to him, "I didn't survive Auschwitz for you to marry a shiksa." Do you see her stagnating? Do you see her ego dissolving in self-centeredness? Do you want to know her? How do you think her son feels?

Our destination as individuals and as a couple—and then a family and then a neighborhood or nation—may dare to be maturity. Before we get to maturity and its sidekick, cultural proficiency, we need spiritual proficiency. Spiritual preparation is not just the goal of life; it is life. You are always preparing to be the person you were created to be. You never succeed. You become holy in the process, on the road, in the journey. Then you mess up, fall off your path, and try again.

Self-regulation and executive function and full personal agency are all important. They are the ground from which we become generous and grateful. When generativity is achieved, it moves into an integration of our egos and prevents despair. Very few of us are spiritually prepared for spiritual evolution. Some pre-evolved people say things like surviving Auschwitz. Or we reject our queer children. Or we carry coded signs about how white people aren't going to be wiped out. We're not. When we act that way, we get stuck with the devolved, the group that won't survive. When we get to a generative cultural proficiency, we build good soil. We evolve.

Many of these matters were predicted by Jesus, who was as scientific as Darwin. He overthrew the rulers of the temples to give God's Spirit and his Spirit a chance. Idolatry is often understood as the only thing God can't forgive. That is stated in the second chapter of Genesis. Other faiths consistently say that when God is displaced and replaced that God gets pissed. Trouble follows. Not that God punishes so much as that we self-punish. We miss the mark of our true humanity. We make ourselves more than we are, which ends up also making us less than we are. We deny the possibility of intimacy with the divine—with God, Allah, Jesus, Christ, Spirit, Force, Energy, Cosmos, Higher Power. We get off track. We get lost. We become homeless. Martin Luther defined sin as *incurvatus in se*, curved in on ourselves, such that we forget how to love, so self-centered and centering are we.

Just because most religion is idolatrous and fundamentally mistaken does not mean that all religion is. If you really want a challenge, try creating a spiritual community for yourself. Try living without one first. You do need validation of your fundamental values. You can't do *anything* alone. But you can dedicate yourself to being a renegade religionist. Why not?

Here is an example of my alter ego, the Dolly Mama, who is trying to develop an alternative way of being spiritual. Her method is an advice column. It has as its objective getting over herself.

Dear Dolly,

I always wanted to be a female Stephen Colbert or female Jon Stewart or at least prevent bias in the hiring of famous comedians. Comics are either a guy, a Catholic, or a Jew. Post-Protestants need not apply. I am the funniest person no one knows about. I am also female, part of the tradition known as "what do women want anyway." I qualify for outsider, underrepresented, even affirmative action, to the world of comedy.

Instead of achieving my goal, I have remained an irreverent reverend, a religious imposter, a career vagabond, an ideological contortionist, a bipartisan compromiser, a political pontificator, a twig gatherer, chic peasant, vine grower, pig breeder, egg gatherer, and daring dilettante. I dance a spiritual jitterbug. Even my parents wonder if I will ever find a secure income or what they call a vocation. I told them I would be a good priest and they weren't happy about that. They knew about me and celibacy. I did marry a Jew, decades ago, in an act of fidelity so widely doubted that many are still holding on to their wedding cards and gifts, just in case. And I like to work on the edge of religious institutions. The pay is terrible but the material is fantastic. You can make good money as a youth worker. You work every Sunday night and play a lot of hide-and-seek in empty church buildings. You also have to come up with one fund raiser after another.

I once started a youth-run composting project in Tucson in a church parking lot. The kids named it "Holy Shit," just to get me in trouble with their parents and my boss, the pastor. It was very successful, both as a fundraiser and a troublemaker. Old ladies in hats carried two lettuce leaves and three teaspoons of coffee grounds in what they called a baggie to church. They then daintily dropped it in the compost, before church. Some of them wore white gloves. The youth group charged a dollar a bag for the compost that "finished" in about two weeks. Celibates, even

117

some old ladies, wouldn't get jokes about finishing. I still tell them just to see who is listening.

We always sold out the bagged compost with its attractive, irreverent label, "HOLY SHIT," in cursive. Sometimes, we got grass clippings from lawn mowers, refusing any grass clippings that looked so good that it probably had chemicals in it. The group made $6000 one year in funds for their "urban plunge" to San Francisco. There we visited the morgue as our first stop, lived in shelters, and ate in soup kitchens. We were doing Bible study that way, looking at life from the bottom up, the way Jesus did. Those were not the funny parts.

The funnier parts were like when one of the kids, a horsewoman, picked up the hundred-pound bag of sand during our visit to the San Francisco police station, after the officer told us that "women can't be cops because they can't pass the test to become one. It requires carrying this bag a hundred feet in a straight line." Our horsewoman just up and did what he told her women couldn't do. She carried the bag on her shoulder in a straight line for one hundred feet. Women became eligible for cop jobs soon after. The year was something like 1974. It wasn't because of our young horsewoman, but she didn't hurt her chance at justice in her bout with prejudice and bias. Even the mistaken potbellied sergeant was amused.

The kids also had a surplus of $750 at the end of the week, after prepaying all the gas for the large rental van's trip home. I was the driver, in an act no insurance company should ever have underwritten. There were nine kids in the van. They sang songs and arm wrestled all the way to and from San Francisco.

The matter of the $750 surplus became the real learning moment for the trip. One of the kids came from a family that had gone out to dinner at the Top of the Mark, a fancy restaurant on a great hill overlooking San Francisco. He argued we should splurge after a week of rice and beans. The more "Christian kids" were appalled.

Dolly, I just didn't know what to do. Wouldn't that kind of extravagance destroy all our learning in one stroke? How would we explain it to the little old ladies in the gloves? What would Jesus do? I agonized for a full day. And still regret our decision to do the splurge. Will Jesus ever forgive me?

Spiritual but Not Religious Comedienne

Dear Spiritual but Not Religious Comedienne,
Of course, Jesus would forgive you for ordering Chateau briand at the Top of the Mark and that very expensive wine you also ordered. The larger issue is not your leading young people astray as a youth worker. Cursing in public is also a problem for people like you, but we will leave the holy shit matter to finer minds.

What Jesus may not appreciate is your overall attitude. You sound ungrateful for problems. You sound overly serious about $750. You sound like your objective in life is to be right or moral or both. You also sound a little bored, which is a very good aptitude in a comedian or comedienne, less so in a Christian. Christians are enthusiastic about life, not bored. So many souls, so many bags of compost! Six thousand by my count. So much shit. Way to go!

You likely have a "mighty fire shut up in your bones," what my therapist calls dynamite up your ___. My therapist is less eloquent than Jeremiah 20:9.

Acedia is what the monks call it. A spiritual boredom, the kind that comes after the twenty-eighth dinner party ends with the same conversation about Hillary as the last one did.

Enthusiasm is downright evangelical. It's an intention to be so full of praise that you are constantly amusing yourself, no matter what anybody else is doing. Go for it. Enthusiasm is a spirituality, just like gratitude. It is like being a cimarron, a formerly caged animal that is allowed to go free. Enthusiasm doesn't stop boredom, but it challenges it every now and then. I hate to tell you but even being on a stage or in a sitcom or on a TV show doesn't cure boredom. I did start collecting my social insecurity and never lost the boredom. I did debate O'Reilly on immigration and he quoted scripture at me. I named my cats interesting names, but no one really cared. Kobe (whom I had to switch to Kofe, due to Kobe Bryant's indiscretions), Hudson, Sampson, and Chewbacca, then the latest, Rip Van Twinkle. I often played in the Miami Senior Wimbledon, also known as Nursing Home Open. I took a three-month sabbatical and every day thought about doing some e-mails after my morning walk, morning coffee, morning swim, morning nap. You get the drift; it was genuine drift. I had a restaurant in Port-au-Prince named after me. I took the sleeper car to New Orleans on the Crescent. I am still as bored as ever, even with wide-spread epistemological insurgency, the ongoing faith crisis in the American people, about which you did nothing even with the spiritually based composting project. It actually sounds like you contributed to it by a self-righteous, high-minded kind of thinking. Why not let the kids have a little fun?

I recommend you live a life that entertains yourself first. Then others. That will be the golden rule of comedy. You can do it. Forget bias. Forget cleverness. Never forget your youth or that great if unholy meal at the Top of the Mark.

Dolly

As you see, Dolly rarely stays long on any one subject. Being spiritually prepared is not a curriculum. It's not even a rite of passage. It is a way of looking at life with God-centered eyes and wondering how to make God laugh.

QUESTIONS TO PONDER AND PRACTICAL APPROACHES

1. Since you as an individual can do anything you want to do with your lonely socially mandated freedom, what might motivate

you to build and join a spiritual community or to make your spiritual values fundamental to your marriage partnership?

2. Have you been disappointed by spiritual communities?

3. Have you been encouraged by spiritual communities? What is the balance between disappointment and encouragement?

4. What difference might you make in that balance ongoing?

5. So far what I have done is to tease you into thinking about marriage differently. I've been hoping you could add the category of spiritual to your preparation for getting married, lest you get into deep water, get in over your head, even drown. Marriage is a serious spiritual matter as well as a serious psychological matter. When you add the category of spiritual to the category of psychological, you don't discount the psychological so much as you enrich it.

6. You may have been enchanted by the notion of queer theology or queer thinking at one point or another. Queer is cohesive thinking. It refuses binaries. It doesn't think that anything is "just" this or that. It imagines that we are all blends of genders, all good and bad, all complete and incomplete, all enthused and bored some of the time or happy and totally frustrated simultaneously. I am inviting you to think queer about religion and then about marriage.

7. So many of us are so spiritually unprepared for the promises of marriage. We make promises we can't keep and we don't even know why we can't keep them or failed to keep them or don't really want to keep them. I am flirting with you here. I am wondering if you could think spiritually and also open your heart to the possibility that the material alone is insufficient ground for the fun we could be having in marriage. By material I mean the reductionism that assumes everything is either sociological, economic, or psychological. Everything, by the way, *is* all of these things and that's not all that everything is. The sum, the total, the parts of "everything" have a spiritual dimension. It doesn't like to be ignored. It will show up in your failures, and

you will have fewer failures if you live a more spiritual life. Or maybe the same number, but you will look at them differently. You will see them as learning experiences or what Dolly calls AFLE, another frigging learning experience.

Appendix

Wedding Services and Premarital Guidance

WHAT KIND OF WEDDING SERVICE SHOULD YOU HAVE WHILE becoming spiritually prepared?

A lot of people call and ask if I will officiate their wedding service. Being a transitional person, I usually say yes and do a traditional service but in a very minimalist way. I love doing weddings that involve several cultural backgrounds. My favorites are "his Jewish mother and Christian father joining her Hindu mother and Brazilian father." Or the Jewish lawyer and Chinese lawyer or the Buddhist and Muslim men.

In the premarital counseling, which I strongly suggest (and lose business suggesting), there are six sessions. The last is the service. Many want to do it first. I compromise more often on four sessions because people really have so much less time. But look at the issues that exist before the service and see if you agree, in principle, that these sessions might help make a marriage of any kind, inside or outside of a tradition, better and more clear and fun.

First, examine your parents' marriage. It will show up in yours. I want to examine which aspect of the lover's parent they are marrying or not marrying. In time I also get to the grandparents. Trust is the issue.

The most normal problems in marriage involve the in-laws. In Yiddish they are called the *Machateynista*. We are joining two families in genetic and financial intimacy. The parents are losing a child. The child is losing the parents. There is a lot of psychological density in marriage. The in-laws may not like each other and may not even know that they don't like each other. It is tremendously important for them to meet before the wedding. If not, there are problems just sitting around unacknowledged, waiting to burst out from under the table and take a center seat.

Second, differences of race, class origin, class current, religious background, ethnic orientation, political affiliation, age, and other factual matters will make the ordinary levels of conflict larger, not smaller. These differences matter. They should be discussed early as they will surely be discussed louder and more often over time.

Third, if there are previous partners, how did things end? How over is the relationship? My antenna almost always goes up around "rebound" marriages, when people are remarrying after less than a year of divorce.

Fourth, matters of money, sex, and power are very important to me. Who has the erotic power? Who initiates lovemaking the most? Who controls the money? As I argue here, the purpose of marriage is to increase, over time, the personal power of each partner. Love is the interest in increasing the other's power. If there are already power imbalances in the relationship, they are likely to persist. I want people well educated in each other's patterns before they walk down the aisle.

Fifth, who wants children and who doesn't? How many? Are they to sleep in the parents' bed or their own bed? What if one of them is stillborn? Children are often considered the point of marriage. People are very likely to have differences about how to raise them. Premarital counseling can help sort this out before disappointment or disagreement sets in.

As part of the premarital, which ranges from 2 to 12 sessions, I often give an assignment. What will be your biggest problem in five years? How will it be connected to your histories? During the third session, we discuss their prophecies. By then we are bonded and are having a good time. These sessions are not designed to resolve the coming problems so much as to name and forecast them. When they show up at the breakfast table, no one will be surprised.

After these sessions, as I said, hopefully six, maybe four, we focus on the service. I have already handed out a template for it. The couple then provides input into the categories.

There are ten liturgically connected parts:

A welcome

A blessing by the family: To the Blood relatives, parents, even if there are two moms and two dads.

Once the bride and groom are in the room, the whole congregation is standing, the officiant says please be seated and says "In the name of all that is good and true and beautiful, in the name of all that has come before and will come after, in the name of True Spirit and Holy Worth, we welcome you. You may also want to name those absent at this point, the deceased . . . grandparents or whatever. Make sure you get the names exactly right.

Then the officiant says: "You came here as one person, you will leave as another. That is the point of liturgy and ritual. It is only right that we ask the people here gathered to join the ritual in blessing you. Will the blood families please rise, parents, siblings and grandparents? " They stand. Officiant asks "Is it your desire to add your blessing to the holy promises about to be made? If so, please announce, this is our desire.

Remain standing.

A blessing by the gathered community: Will the friends of both the bride and groom (or man and man or woman and woman or thems in some way they choose to be addressed) join the family in addiing their blessing.

Please rise.

Is it your desire to add your blessing to the promises about to
be made? If so announce, with joy and acclamation, THIS
IS OUR DESIRE.

The Bride and groom are looking at the congregation as
these blessings proceed.

Usually this is their first hankie moment. It also relaxes the
entire room as everybody now has done something.

The service proceeds.

Some music

A reading or two or three

The promises

The vows

The rings

The announcement

The kiss

It often takes longer at the rehearsal to deal with the entrances
and the exits than it does with the service. Why? Because the
drama and narrative arc of the wedding are in the coming in as one
person and leaving as another. The language matters less than the
liturgy, the pattern, the motion toward each other. There are two
hankie moments in the service. One is the accelerating blessings
of the family and friends, right at the top, where the couple looks
at their gathered community and feels their support and blessing.
The second is when they kiss. Orchestration of the kiss with the
musician is my job; kissing is theirs.

Often, I invoke God beyond God at the beginning, "the one
whom no one can name, the one whom some call Allah, and others, Jesus, whom some call Ruach and others Yahweh, whom some
call Spirit or Energy or Force or Creator, whom others cannot

comprehend, nevertheless, thou beyond any human captivity or naming, draw near."

If asked early in the premarital sessions for permission to include God, the couple might say no. I usually find a way to sneak it in or to say something in universal language, like "Power greater than ours," or some such universal reach for the transcendent that doesn't sound religious.

Glitches do occur. One couple realized at the last session that she wanted to have a full set of matching dishes and he thought the hodgepodge they had was just fine. He wants to use the gift registry to send money to an international aid organization. I invited them to talk to their parents about this obvious difference in housekeeping and daily living. Her mother had matching dishes, a service for eight; his did not. This process brought the four parents into an advisory role for the marriage and the parents loved it. They were honored . . . and they became better in-laws.

The lost preparation in a world where religious meanness and stupidity prevails and is dominant seriously undermines the problem of secularization, caused by the moral injury of stupid and mean religion.

Romantic consumerism is the decision to stop shopping. More important than the promise of fidelity, "cleaving only unto you as long as we both shall live." Seventy years is a long time to have sex with only one person.

Notes

Chapter 1
1. Erica Panday, "America the Single," Axios, February 25, 2023.
2. Ibid.
3. Ibid.
4. Ibid.
5. Ibid.

Chapter 2
1. David Brooks, *New York Times*, September 27, 2020.
2. David Brooks, "The Nuclear Family Was a Mistake," *Atlantic*, March 2020.

Chapter 3
1. Barry Kosmin, *Research Report: The National Survey of Religious Identification 1989–1990* (New York: CUNY Graduate School of University Center, 1991).
2. Elizabeth Drescher, "Nones by Many Other Names: The Religiously Unaffiliated in the News, 18th to 20th Century," Oxford Handbooks Online, December 5, 2014, accessed December 3, 2019, https://www-oxfordhandbooks-com.dtl.idm.oclc.org/view/10.1093/oxfordhb/9780199935420.001.0001/oxfordhb-9780199935420-e-16.
3. Robert D. Putnam and David E. Campbell, *American Grace: How Religion Divides and Unites Us* (New York: Simon & Schuster, 2010), 132.
4. Putnam and Campbell, *American Grace*, 91–133. (This passage was also used in a previous paper I wrote for the DMin Seminar II.)
5. Putnam and Campbell, *American Grace*, 91.
6. Joel Thiessen and Sarah Wilkins-Laflamme, "Becoming a Religious None: Irreligious Socialization and Disaffiliation," *Journal for the Scientific Study of Religion* 56, no. 1 (2017): 77, 79.
7. Robert P. Jones, Daniel Cox, Betsy Cooper, and Rachel Lienesch, *Exodus: Why Americans Are Leaving Religion—and Why They're Unlikely to Come Back* (Washington, DC: Public Religion Research Institute, September 22, 2016), 8–9.

Chapter 5
1. Helen Lewis, "Where Is Our Paradise of Guilt-Free Sex?," *Atlantic*, October 2021.
2. Lewis, "Guilt-Free Sex."
3. Rom. 12:1 (New International Version 1984).

4. Luis Alberto Urrea, Borders are Limited Spaces, August 26, 2021, https://onbeing.org.

5. June 2021 The book was compiled by Vincent Mongaillard, published by Editions de l'Opportun.

6. Ibid.

7. NIV 1984.

Chapter 6

1. Alain de Botton, "Alain de Botton on Romanticism," School of Life, July 30, 2016, YouTube video, 2:49, https://www.youtube.com/watch?v=sPOuIyEJnbE.

Chapter 7

1. Matthew Schneier, "The Return of FOMO," The Cut, June 7, 2021, https://www.thecut.com/2021/06/the-return-of-fomo.html.

Chapter 8

1. *Harry Potter and the Sacred Text* podcast, accessed December 3, 2019, http://www.harrypottersacredtext.com/methodology.

2. Paul T. Corrigan, "Postsecular Young Adult Literature," in *Teens and the New Religious Landscape: Essays on Contemporary Young Adult Fiction*, ed. Jacob Stratman (Jefferson, NC: McFarland, 2018), 17.

3. Discussed in Jacob Stratman, "The Customized Religion: Moralistic Therapeutic Deism, American Teenagers and Pete Hautman's *Godless*," in *Teens and the New Religious Landscape: Essays on Contemporary Young Adult Fiction*, ed. Jacob Stratman (Jefferson, NC: McFarland, 2018), 112.

4. Barry Kosmin, *Research Report: The National Survey of Religious Identification 1989–1990* (New York: CUNY Graduate School of University Center, 1991).

INDEX

community: imperfection and, 110; of practice, 94–95; queer, 79; spiritual, 99, 103, 105, 107–8, 120–21; in wedding, 125
confession, 52–53
conflict, 3, 124; learning from, 98, 106–8; love and, 85
confusion: moral, 40; spiritual, 36–37, 73
connection, control and, 91–93
consensual intimacy, 61–62
consumerism, romantic, 126
control, connection and, 91–93
coronavirus. *See* COVID-19
counseling, premarital, 123–26
covenant, 43–44, 55
COVID-19, 13–15, 21–22, 77
creativity, adjustment and, 106
criteria, for dating and marriage, 7–8
cultural proficiency, 3, 28–29, 114–15
culture, 34–36; God in, 12–13; learning of, 16–17, 29, 76, 87–89
cynicism, about marriage, 24–26

Dalai Lama, 102
Darwin, Charles, 116
date night: with God, 94–95; romance and, 67–68
date rape, 74

dating, 7–8, 71–74
Dear Dolly, 56–62, 117–20
death, 13; of child, 72; of in-laws, 80; of spouse, 101
decision-making, elders and, 80–81
deconversion, religious, 37–39, 98
demographics, changes in, 114
development, emotional, 115
difference, 79; history and, 104
dilution, of religion, 77
disaffiliation: affiliation and, 37–40, 98; grief and, 40–41
distraction, 56–58
diversity, 64, 102; bidding and, 66; dating and, 71–72, 74; intimate, 1–2, 4; training for, 87–89
divine, 88–89, 116
divorce, 6, 9, 83; affairs and, 89–90; blame and, 75–76, 86; in interfaith marriages, 4, 86; religious deconversion and, 98; stigma of, 87; suffering and, 84–85; surnames and, 27–28
Dolly Mama, 42, 102, 106–11, 116, 121–22; Dear Dolly, 56–62, 117–20
Dworkin, Andrea, 59

Edelman, Marian, 32
education, sex, 60–61
Einstein, Albert, 15
elders, decision-making and,
 80–81. *See also* in-laws
Ellis Island, 77
emotional development, 115
emotions, sex and, 59–62
empowerment, sex and, 55
enthusiasm, 119–20
Erikson, Erik, 115
erotic moments, 57–58
eschatology, 101
ethnicity, race and, 7, 71, 73,
 85, 88, 124
evaluation, by bidding, 67
"external pluralism," "internal
 pluralism" and, 72–73

Facebook, 95
failure, 86, 121–22; divorce
 and, 84
fake it till you make it, 109
falling, in love, 4, 16–17,
 24–25, 61
false gods, 17
family: blended, 20, 75–77;
 boundaries with, 68–69;
 chosen, 23–24; fights in,
 11, 87, 90; marriage to,
 75–76, 79; nuclear, 22–23,
 68, 80; queer community
 and, 79; two-career, 25–26
Faulkner, William, 77

feminism, 25
Fiddler on the Roof, 8
fidelity, 49–51, 126
fights, 12; in families, 11, 87,
 90; trust and, 69
Finkel, Eli, 24
firsts, relationship, 101–2; "first
 date" story, 64
Foote, Shelby, 32
forever, 5–6, 13, 20–21
forgiveness, 10, 84–86, 88, 119
foundations, in relationships,
 34–36, 53
Frankl, Viktor, 12
friendships, 34–35, 67–68,
 78–79, 95
fun, 26, 55, 65, 68, 111, 120–21
fundamental values, 116
funerals, 46
future, 5, 109; tradition and,
 26, 78, 81, 88, 105–6

Gallup poll, 103
gay, lesbian, bisexual,
 transgender, and queer
 (GLBTQ), 28–29. *See also*
 queer
gay marriage, 19
genealogy, 102–3
generations, marriage and, 7,
 23–24
generativity, 115–16
Gilman, Charlotte Perkins,
 19, 24

GLBTQ. *See* gay, lesbian, bisexual, transgender, and queer
goals, 3, 65, 85, 101, 115
God, 4, 16; belonging to, 77; in culture, 12–13; date night with, 94–95; beyond God, 125–26; in interfaith marriages, 45; love and, 11, 47, 54, 89; no mention of, 10–11, 43–45; partnership with, 42, 47, 53; security and, 13–14; word of, 78
gods, false, 17
Goldberg, Michelle, 59
good, imperfection and, 104–5
The Good Divorce (Ahrons), 55, 87
governance, of self, 108
grief, disaffiliation and, 40–41
guilt, 43, 80–81; blame and, 90–91

habit, 42, 56–57, 88; prayer as, 32–33; of Spirit, 12–13
happiness, in marriage, 3–4, 9, 50, 86, 93
Hartford Seminary, 40–41
heartbreak, 27, 93
Herod, 15, 17
Hindu, 1, 93

history, 97, 102–4; of deconversion, 9–10, 38, 98; problems and, 124–25
holiness, 114–15; marriage and, 24–25, 29, 47, 51, 103, 113
honesty, 81, 95; promise and, 53–54; sex and, 60–62
humility, Jesus and, 96

idolatry, 114, 116; of partner, 12, 53–54
immigrants, 21–22
imperfection, 45; community and, 110; good and, 104–5
impossibility, 45, 110
improvement, rules for, 105–10
India, 1
individualism, 22, 27; choice and, 113; meditation and, 33, 96; secularism and, 21, 26; in US, 10, 13–14
injury, moral, 23, 44, 126
in-laws, 75–76, 78, 126; change and, 16–17, 77, 79; communication with, 81; death of, 80; trust and, 123–24
insurance policy, marriage as, 19, 24–26
interfaith marriages, 7, 37, 40, 114; dating websites and, 71; divorce in, 4, 86; God in, 45

ABOUT THE AUTHOR

Rev. Dr. Donna Schaper is a bridge pastor in Connecticut since arriving from Judson Memorial Church in New York City. She is an associate professor of leadership at Hartford International University and a chaplain at the Silver Linings Corporation. An author of 39 books, her pen name is The Dolly Mama.

CPSIA information can be obtained
at www.ICGtesting.com
Printed in the USA
BVHW040719100423
661985BV00001B/1

9 781538 143520